Angels in Our Hearts

CASEY WATSON & ROSIE LEWIS

Angels in Our Hearts

A moving collection of true fostering stories

HARPER
element

HarperElement
An imprint of HarperCollins*Publishers*
1 London Bridge Street
London SE1 9GF

www.harpercollins.co.uk

Helpless first published by HarperCollins*Publishers* 2013
A Small Boy's Cry first published by HarperElement 2014
Two More Sleeps first published by HarperElement 2014
Unexpected first published by HarperElement 2015
Just a Boy first published by HarperElement 2013
At Risk first published by HarperElement 2016

This edition HarperElement 2019

18 19 20 21 22 LSC 10 9 8 7 6 5 4 3 2 1

© Rosie Lewis 2013, 2014, 2015, 2018
© Casey Watson. 2013, 2016, 2018

Rosie Lewis and Casey Watson assert the moral right
to be identified as the authors of this work

A catalogue record of this book is
available from the British Library

ISBN 978-0-00-830595-6

Printed and bound in the United States of America

For more information visit: www.harpercollins.co.uk/green

Contents

Introduction
by Casey Watson

It is such an honour to be able to share these pages with fellow foster carer and author, Rosie Lewis. Not only are her stories inspiring for you all to read, but they continue to inspire me. As a carer for many years I know that all children are very different and come from very different backgrounds, so there are no hard and set rules for looking after them. Fostering can often seem like an isolating job, and there are days when you feel that you've emptied your tool box and have nothing left to work with. These moments, thankfully, are fleeting, and somewhere, from the depths of our hearts, we always manage to find some clarity – and then it's sleeves rolled up and business as usual.

Reading Rosie's stories makes me realise that although all the children may be different, the trials and tribulations of fostering are universal. We love, we nurture and we try to find the key to a child's happiness – or at least the key that unlocks their demons – and then we can try help to break them down and pave the way to the future. What is similar about Rosie and myself is that we both understand what a rollercoaster our career choice has been, but we take the knocks, the red tape and the teenage angst in our stride and we try to see the lighter side. I'm certain that Rosie would agree with me that sometimes, if we didn't laugh, we would cry – but this only serves to make us stronger.

I'm sure you will enjoy these short snapshots into our daily lives, and I'm delighted to introduce Rosie Lewis.

I dedicate this book to the children who have found themselves a place in our home over the years, and taught us more than we could ever teach them. I'd also like to spare a thought for all the dedicated social workers out there who work so hard to make a difference and rarely get any credit. And finally, to all the foster carers, adopters and readers who care so much – as Casey says, hats off to you all!

Rosie

ROSIE LEWIS

Helpless

A True
Short Story

Helpless

'Course, I seen it all, love,' Bob, my police escort, says as we drive through the cold November night towards the hospital. 'Twisted car wrecks, stab victims, the lot, but I couldn't do what you do, not for twice my police pension.'

Smiling, I re-check the contents of the hurriedly packed nappy bag on my lap, mentally running through the items I might need to get through the next twenty-four hours. Bob's reaction isn't surprising. Who wouldn't be overwhelmed by the prospect of being permanently on duty? When I'm fostering, every second of my existence is dominated by the needs of the damaged child, but I don't mind. Like many foster carers, I'm driven by a powerful need to ease their pain.

I remember myself as a child, walking by our local newsagents on the way to school. Outside the shop stood a little wooden figure of a beggar boy with polio, both legs fixed in metal callipers and a forlorn expression painted on his face. He held up a sign saying 'Please give' and there was a slot in the top of his head for pennies. Undeterred by the bird droppings across his shoulders, I would give him a quick hug, longing to take him home and make him better.

My pulse quickens as we pass over a deserted bridge lined with old-fashioned street-lamps. After seven years of fostering I still feel an intense excitement when taking on a new child. It's only been a few days since my last placement ended and already I'm itching to fill the void.

As we drive past the riverside council blocks I'm reminded of one of my previous charges – three-year-old Connor, a boy who spent a large part of his day roaming the second floor of the grim building with his overfull nappy hanging at his knees while his mother familiarised herself with a string of violent, resentful partners. How fragile their lives are, I think, when nothing is certain and the events of one day can turn everything familiar upside down.

Soon we turn into a main road and the functional, rectangular building of the city hospital looms into view. Bob pulls the police car into the large parking area outside the maternity wing and I reach for the infant seat with trembling fingers, gripped by a sudden fear that I'm too out of practice to care for such a young baby.

Coming in from the knife-like wind, the warmth of the maternity unit engulfs me like a blanket. Another police officer stands guard outside the delivery suite and the sight causes my stomach to flip. What if the birth family find out where I live? Am I putting my own children at risk?

Bob seems to sense my apprehension, gently cupping my elbow and leading the way to reception. I show the midwife, a young but harassed-looking woman, my ID card. 'I'll call Sister for you,' she says, checking her bleeper and hurrying off down the equipment-lined corridor.

My stomach churns as I pace the stark white corridors like an expectant father from another era, back in the days when convention kept men out of the delivery suite. A faint cry and the rhythmic thud of sensible shoes signals another breathless charge of adrenaline. Craning my neck, I catch a glimpse of Sister as she rounds the corner, a small, ruffled blanket in her arms. The weak cry gradually increases in volume until it sounds like an ailing but furious kitten. I suddenly feel light-headed and realise that I'm holding my breath.

'Hello, dear,' the middle-aged woman says, raising her voice to compete with the mewing. She lifts her glasses and squints at the ID badge hanging around my neck. 'I'm told you're a specialist carer?'

I nod, biting my lower lip. When I took the call at midnight from my fostering agency there was no mention of the need for specialised care. My pulse rises again, wondering what could be wrong – HIV? Hepatitis? I know from experience that foster carers are sometimes the last to find out such vital information.

Sister leans in conspiratorially. 'We'd generally hang onto the poor mite for a bit longer but, well, you've probably been told, the family are making all sorts of threats.'

I nod again. Foster carers are often required to liaise with intimidating and hostile parents but tight budgets don't usually stretch to the luxury of police escorts.

'I suspect little Sarah has the tail end of something nasty in her system. We're not entirely sure what Mum was on, though she claims to be teetotal.'

Don't they all? I marvel, my heart sinking like a lift with a snapped cable. If she is withdrawing there'll be a tough time ahead. For a split-second I wonder at my choice of career, until I feel her warm weight in the crook of my left arm. I'm taken aback by how light she feels, as if there's nothing wrapped in the blanket but air.

Momentarily disorientated by the move, the baby stops shrieking and blinks around in surprise. The skin on her face is wrinkled and reddish. Milky eyes return my stare, narrowed pupils betraying the harsh substances running through her veins. Her expression is filled with a puzzlement that says, 'Am I safe with you?'

Without warning she winces and her eyes screw up, the crescent of lashes disappearing with a wail of desperation. Her chin trembles, tiny fingers balling into tight fists. I begin to sway, aware of a grinding ache in my solar plexus; a longing to soothe the pain from her brow.

Slipping my right forefinger into her clammy palm I make shushing noises. 'It's going to be alright,' I whisper, my heart lurching.

'Has she been given any methadone?' I ask, without taking my gaze away from her tiny face.

Sister shakes her head. 'We'd need to keep her in the special care unit for that and the paediatrician thinks she may just get away with it,' she squeezes my arm, 'with a lot of TLC.'

Twenty minutes later I unwind the hospital blanket and dress her in a thick all-in-one coat. Without the stiff swaddling she feels almost weightless, like a terrifyingly vulnerable life-like doll. Her limbs flop in my hands like cooked noodles and I have to take a few deep breaths to calm myself as I set the baby car seat on the floor and secure the straps around her; they seem far too harsh and unforgiving against someone so small and precious. She slumps over, still screeching piteously and I picture her curled up in her mother's womb, where, even there, she wasn't safe.

An icy wind hits me as I leave the warm building. I make soothing noises as I secure Sarah's baby seat in the rear of the squad car but it doesn't help – she howls constantly and with rising desperation. The sound sets off a siren in my mind flashing the message, 'DO SOMETHING!' By the time we pull into our quiet suburban street I'm frantic to get her out and hold her to me – anything to stop the crying.

After thanking Bob, I scramble up the path, surprised to find the front door yanked open in a fever of excitement and anticipation as my children, Emily and Jamie, rush to catch a first glimpse of their new housemate.

My mother hovers behind, as eager as they are to meet her new temporary foster granddaughter. She is one of my registered 'back-up carers' and only lives a few minutes away by car, a godsend on nights like this when I have to leave the house without much notice.

'Ah, look, she's so tiny!' My sixteen-year-old daughter lifts Sarah from her seat like a seasoned professional, gently moving the screaming baby to a position over her shoulder and performing an instinctive little dance. Sarah's cries weaken as her tummy is cradled against her foster sister's warmth.

Half an hour later, Emily and Jamie reluctantly head off back to bed, Sarah still bawling as my mother cradles her in her lap. 'Put a drop of brandy in her bottle, that'll settle her,' she suggests.

'I can't do that, Mum!' She has no idea of the fall-out if social services even heard those words pass her lips.

'Don't look like that,' she says defensively. 'I'm only joking. Not that it ever did you lot any harm.'

Rolling my eyes, I swoop the baby up and try to tempt her with a dummy, knowing that sucking will help to ease her stomach cramps. Her lips are as tiny as two petals and surrounded by small blisters, the damage from her harsh screams. Fear grips my insides; what if she refuses to ever stop crying? Her voice is already hoarse. Mum warms one of the glass bottles of milk from the hospital, passing it to me.

'You haven't slipped any tea in there, have you?'

'Course not, but you used to love a drop of tea,' she says over the din. 'Couldn't get enough of it.'

Scoffing, I offer Sarah the milk, grateful for the reprieve as she guzzles hungrily. Mum leans over to watch and we exchange smiles at the cute little swallowing noises she makes.

After taking almost an ounce she falls into an exhausted sleep in my arms, her mouth still attached to the teat. I thank Mum then carefully creep up the stairs, terrified that her eyes will pop open the second I lay her in the hastily constructed crib beside my bed. She whimpers when I withdraw my arms, pulling her legs up to her chest. Even while sleeping, she is clearly in pain.

Switching off the light, I step out of my clothes and leave them in a discarded heap on the floor. Reaching blindly down to the crib, I pop Sarah's dummy back in for the umpteenth time and slip quietly under my duvet. It has been a long night and, although tired, I feel a profound sense of fulfilment. Before fostering I didn't quite understand where I belonged. Listening to Sarah's gentle whimpers as she snoozes in the crib beside me lifts my heart. It is a matchless sensation, reminding me that I've found the job that fits me best. Despite the frustrations, interrupted sleeps and endless paperwork, I wouldn't have it any other way.

Twelve minutes later Sarah is screaming again, a piercing high-pitched wail that signals intense pain, not hunger. I lift her from her crib and notice tiny beads of sweat forming on her forehead. Her lower lip trembles and her limbs flail wildly as I cradle her in my arms and hold her close.

Re-adjusting my pillows against the headboard I lean back, cuddling her against my chest. It's a position my own children relaxed in when they were newborns but Sarah remains so agitated that I have to get up, walk around the bedroom and bob her gently up and down. Her harsh cries subside into little sobs and I begin to fear that her birth mother's drug of choice may have been crack. It would explain the rigidity in her muscles, the pain etched onto her tiny features.

The rest of the night passes in a blur as I continuously walk the length of my bedroom, trying to console her. As winter sunlight creeps into the room she finally settles and I ease her into her crib, dummy in position and tightly swaddled. Padding to the kitchen, I reach for the coffee jar like a drowning woman to a dinghy. I'm grateful when my mother offers to feed Sarah if she wakes, allowing me the time to write up my daily record sheet and prepare bottles for the next twenty-four hours. It feels surreal to be sterilising feeding equipment again.

My whole body aches with tension as I wave Emily and Jamie off to school a couple of hours later. Tiredness makes me feel like I'm wading through petroleum jelly and by mid-morning, as my mother gathers her bags, I feel a moment's panic at being left alone with Sarah.

Mum brushes a kiss on my cheek. 'Talk later. I hope she settles for you.'

I'm tempted to grip her arm and plead with her to stay but I remind myself that I'm nearly forty, not a teenaged first-time mum. 'I'm sure we'll be fine,' I say, smiling with a confidence I don't feel.

* * *

We spend the rest of the morning walking from the front door to the kitchen and then back again, interrupted only by regular pit-stops at the kettle to warm her bottles. She seems to drink more if she sucks while we stroll; I think the movement distracts her from the painful cramps in her stomach. By 1 p.m. nausea sets in and I realise that I haven't eaten for hours. Lunch is a few hurried handfuls of nuts and a clumsily buttered piece of bread, eaten as we complete yet another circuit of the kitchen.

Emily willingly takes the baton and makes laps of the house when she gets in from school so that I can toss a quick stir-fry together.

'It won't be like this for ever,' I reassure Emily and Jamie as they eat. 'In a few weeks she'll be rolling around the carpet and cooing at us.'

'We know Mum, don't worry.'

With fostering, there are times when my attention is stretched a little too thinly and, I muse with a twinge of guilt, we have experienced a number of difficult placements over the years. Kissing their heads, I remind myself that there are lots of positives for birth children in fostering families and at least I'm around for them at the end of the school day.

Before her last bottle I attempt a shower. Securing Sarah in her bouncy chair, I flick the switch to vibrate and carry her to the bathroom. She immediately objects, traumatised by the separation. In record speed I remove my clothes and jump into the steamy hot jets, her howls already at fever pitch. Within seconds her face is purple and she's reached the holding breath stage so I stumble out and wriggle into my dressing gown even though I'm still soaking wet.

We both sigh with relief when she's back in my arms, her ear pressed against my heart. With pyjamas damp and twisted, I climb into bed, Sarah's tiny ribs vibrating against mine as her sobs subside. The arm she is resting on falls asleep but she is so peaceful that I dare not move to get the blood flowing. Barely twenty minutes later she starts to howl again, the muscles in her tiny body trembling violently.

By 3 a.m. I shiver with exhaustion as I offer her a third bottle in as many hours. She only seems able to take half an ounce or so at a time, her stomach making sounds like mini-explosions as she feeds. Sinking my head back, I close my eyes and pray for some reprieve, only to be woken minutes later by an inordinate volume of milk soaking my chest. How she manages to bring so much up I'll never fathom, with her taking so little in.

Back on my feet, I pace the room but this time even movement won't soothe her. Her piercing shrieks addle my brain and I start to panic, until it occurs to me to sing.

My voice croaky from tiredness, I stand at the window with Sarah in my arms and sing 'Hush, Little Baby'. I didn't even realise I knew all the words. Serenading the empty moonlit street, I wonder if I'm the only person awake in the whole of the north of England. My head thuds with exhaustion and I sing with my eyes half-open, just enough to make out her shape through my eyelashes. I'm surprised to find her watching me with a little frown, as if she's trying to make sense of every tuneless word.

As she clenches a tight hold of my finger and locks eyes with mine, I'm filled with renewed confidence that we'll both get through this ordeal just fine.

When I wake at 5:30 a.m. the low thud in my head has become a throbbing pain, my crusty eyes aching. I catch a glimpse of myself in the bathroom mirror and quickly look away, deciding my time will be far better spent trying to make the house look neater than attempting the mammoth task of tidying myself up. Desmond, my supervising social worker, and Sue, Sarah's own social worker, are visiting this morning for the placement planning meeting and I want to appear as if I'm in full control. After waving my own children off to school I scan the living room, hardly knowing where to start. I'd forgotten how someone so little can cause such an inordinate amount of chaos.

Tucking her nappies and wipes in the magazine rack, my back strains with the effort of cleaning with Sarah attached to my chest. I decide to give up and let them take me as they find me. I'll be no use to anyone if my back goes. An hour later, as I make one final effort by sweeping the detritus of the morning into the cupboard under the stairs, the doorbell rings.

'Hi, Desmond,' I say, genuinely pleased to see him. Desmond has been my link worker from the fostering agency ever since I registered, and we quickly established a rapport. Only a few years older than me and with a Scottish lilt to his voice, I feel comfortable in his company and able to speak to him with complete frankness, something I fear I will be unable to do in the presence of the social worker who follows him in.

I have never met Sue before – a tall, formidable-looking woman in her fifties with short, permed black hair. As I welcome them into the living room, Sue fills the space with the scent of her musty perfume. 'Can she breathe in that thing?' she asks, arching her pencilled-in eyebrows at the harness.

She reminds me of my old religious studies teacher, her disapproving voice strained after years of being hugely irritated by unruly children.

'Of course, she's comforted by the closeness and ...' I answer falteringly before trailing off. Sue has sat herself down and is removing a diary from her large canvas bag, not even listening. Desmond raises his eyebrows.

'Well, I can't stay long.' Sue thrusts a copy of the placement agreement towards me and I smile weakly, tiredness minimising my ability for small talk. 'Check through and sign the last page. I need to get back to the office before lunch.'

Within ten minutes and without even asking how the baby is doing, Sue informs me that I must take Sarah for contact with her birth mother in the morning. Then, with a withering expression, she says goodbye.

* * *

Helpless

The next morning I wake to a leaden, cold sky. It rains hard and steady from 5 a.m. and continues incessantly as I drive along unfamiliar country roads and through the black wrought iron gates of the psychiatric hospital. Stumbling through the sodden lawns with Sarah sleeping in the car seat lodged in the crook of my arm, my socks wringing wet and clinging to me, I feel a stab of irritation towards Sue, Sarah's social worker.

During her whirlwind visit she neglected to mention that Sarah's birth mother had been detained under a section of the Mental Health Act 1983 after attacking one of the midwives with her dinner fork. Taking a deep breath to calm myself, I stagger across the sprawling grounds towards the hospital, wondering whether the car-seat manufacturer enjoys a practical joke with its customers by putting rocks in the base of their products. Bare trees cast skeletal shadows across the grounds and rolls of barbed wire atop the high boundary walls are a reminder that the hospital building, a large old country house with ivy-covered red brick, is not the setting for an episode of *Downton Abbey*.

A strong smell of antiseptic hits my nostrils as I enter the cavernous lobby. The receptionist checks my ID and directs me towards the quiet room where I am to meet Sue. A nurse, bespectacled, with a touch of rosacea on her cheeks, gives me a sidelong glance. 'Can I help?' she asks in a slightly suspicious tone, probably wondering why on earth I'd bring a baby to a place like this.

Sue suddenly appears in the corridor, flanked by another member of staff. 'This way,' she trills. The attendant, a stout, short woman with cropped hair, leads the way down another bleak corridor, this one separated by several iron doors. Reaching for the large bunch of keys hanging from her waist band, she turns to us. 'Stay near the door so you've got a quick exit if you need one,' she mouths, ushering us into a side room.

Alarmed, I stare wide-eyed at Sue but she waves her hand. 'It's alright, I'll be right beside you.' Suddenly I find her redoubtable presence hugely reassuring and wonder if I'd be just as forbidding after twenty years doing her job.

The room is small and at the far end an overweight young woman lies face down on a bed. Barely out of her teenage years, she lifts her head slowly as we enter the room, such a delayed reaction that I wonder if she is heavily sedated.

'Morning, Sam,' Sue says, briskly. 'You've only got half an hour's contact so come along, sit yourself up.'

Obediently, Sam rises, her flimsy T-shirt riding up. Deep scarlet stretch marks and sagging skin remind me how recently she gave birth. The young woman glances towards me through a curtain of dark, lank hair with heavy, swollen eyes. She meets my gaze and I smile but she doesn't respond, looking quickly away. From outside I can hear the constant murmur of voices, the occasional sound of running feet. My palms begin to sweat.

'Hello, Sam.' Smiling nervously, I release the baby from her papoose. Sarah immediately objects, drawing her legs to her stomach and yowling. Wary of making any unexpected moves, I glance towards Sue for direction.

'Yes, go on, hand her over,' she says in a tone that tells me she is accustomed to being obeyed.

Gently, I lay Sarah in her mother's waiting arms. A dank, unwashed smell rises from Sam's body and I feel a moment's revulsion. Sarah screams and her mother takes this as a signal of hunger, lifting her T-shirt and releasing one of her pendulous breasts. With armpits raised the smell intensifies and I take a few steps back, forcing myself to focus on an unpleasant-looking stain in the middle of the carpet.

Oblivious to my embarrassment, Sam 'encourages' Sarah to latch on by slapping her over the face with an engorged nipple. Sarah tries to wriggle away from the mammary onslaught, throwing her head wildly from side to side. She yowls piteously, her skin the colour of beetroot.

Sue remains near the doorway, her expression watchful. Sam groans at her baby's refusal to co-operate and I can sense her growing impatience. A vein throbs in my temple as maternal protectiveness roars up in me but I set my jaw and force myself to ignore it. It's easy to forget that I have no rights to this baby. My eyes flick between Sue and Sarah, feeling utterly helpless. The social worker appears too engrossed to perform a rescue, scribbling away in her notebook.

'I have a bottle in my bag if you'd prefer ...' I offer in a quiet voice.

'Oh, for fuck's sake.' Sam releases her grip and Sarah's tiny head, downed with a thatch of hair the same colour as her mother's, lolls back awkwardly. 'Why won't she shut up?' She looks up at me accusingly. ''ere, take her.'

Biting down a sudden spasm of contempt, I take the sobbing baby into my arms and rock to console her. Her sleep suit is damp with perspiration. Had Sam shown some concern for her child, some remorse, I might have felt more empathy. Did she not realise the suffering her addiction had caused?

'Contact suspended for today,' Sue announces, snapping her notebook shut.

Sam stares rigidly ahead as I back towards the door, her face expressionless.

It's funny how quickly our family adjusts to the needs of new arrivals, how normal it all becomes. When Sarah has been with us for almost four weeks, I pick her up from her cot and realise that the wail that was so nauseating in its pitch during her first fortnight has already toned down to an ordinary cry.

Encouraged, once the children leave for school I crank the heating up, then run the bath. Affronted by being undressed, Sarah shrieks, her features crumpling with rage but as I lower her into the warm water, her muscles instantly loosen. Her feet, usually arched in pain, flex and begin to wriggle in the solace of the water. Her legs fall open at the knees and tiny hands stretch to form a starfish.

Wrapped in a towel I take her back downstairs and lay her on the fluffy rug in front of the fire, amazed that she is still lying contentedly despite not being attached to my chest. Rubbing my hands together to warm them, I roll her onto her tummy and her head rests to the side. Confusion crosses her features and she opens her tiny mouth to protest but as I massage the soft skin on her back with gentle fingers she relaxes, expelling a tiny breath of air.

Witnessing Sarah as she blossoms fills me with a sense of achievement, reminding me of the joy I felt a few weeks into my first placement, eight years earlier. I was daunted when the three young siblings arrived. As they sobbed in their beds I buried my face in my hands, almost as bewildered as they were. A few weeks later I realised that trusty old-fashioned love, routine and discipline is often all the expertise that is needed to see a transformation.

When she's dressed and back in her blanket I drop her next feed into a jug of hot water and hold her in my arms at the garden door while we wait for the milk to warm. Her eyes flicker to our horse-chestnut tree, the bare branches swaying in the winter breeze. 'When summer arrives we'll be out there on the grass, warming our feet in the sun,' I tell her as I brush a kiss on her soft cheek and inhale her sweet, infant scent. Rocked by a sudden feeling of déjà vu, I realise she smells the same as my own babies did.

Her hand rises up out of the blanket and searches the air, coming to rest inside the collar of my cardigan. She clenches it and I coo at her, tilting her up to kiss her cheek. With parted lips, her eyes narrow and she bestows a fleeting, crooked smile. A sudden rush of love besieges me. No, don't let yourself, I silently counsel.

* * *

By the end of our fifth week together, when Emily and Jamie leave the house I light the coal fire to bring a bit of cheer into the living room and turn the radio to Smooth FM. Sarah turns her head and watches as the flames sputter into life, her legs scissoring jauntily in response to the music. I'm thrilled. Clearly the drugs in her system haven't adversely affected her hearing.

Bending on all fours, I lift her vest and lean in to kiss her tummy. She gurgles in delight, her pleasure bolstering my decision to reject the safer caring plan presented to me when I first registered as a foster carer. One of the conditions of the plan is that carers must agree never to tickle foster children. I refused, only signing when that particular condition was removed. Several other carers followed suit, in agreement that there are times when tickling is appropriate. Of course, I wouldn't launch myself on a child who may have been sexually abused but why shouldn't a newborn baby know what a raspberry feels like, just because they're a ward of the state?

Worn out by the excitement, she begins to grizzle so I wrap her in a blanket and gather her in my arms, settling the two of us on the sofa. She lies for a few moments looking up at me as I hold her snugly. Watching her eyes flicker, my head drops back and for a few minutes we doze together.

The telephone jerks me awake. Irritated, I reach for the cordless phone with my spare hand.

'Hello?'

'Hi, Rosie.' It's Desmond. He hesitates for a moment and I tense, sensing bad news. Complaints against foster carers are common, particularly when mothers see another woman cradling their own newborn baby.

'Oh dear. Go on, what's up?'

'The local authority is moving Sarah on to other carers, quite soon. Next week in fact.'

'Moving her? Why?' I glance down at her peaceful face, feeling suddenly angry. I had heard of children moving foster placements for financial reasons. Social services make an effort to place their looked after children with locally registered carers but if they are full or they refuse a placement, agency carers are employed. If a local authority carer then becomes available, the child is sometimes moved on, even if they've been settled somewhere for a considerable amount of time. I close my hand around the receiver so tightly that the muscles in my arm begin to ache.

'Don't worry, it's not what you think. The local authority have a couple who have just passed panel and are desperate to adopt a baby. They registered specifically for that reason. The sooner she's settled, the better.'

I feel as if a cold band is clamping around my heart. I know he's right, of course. It will be wonderful for Sarah to get the inevitable move over with while she's so young, so that the new couple are all she'll ever remember. It's a system that has worked well in the US and I had read somewhere that various local authorities were trialling the procedure in the UK. The couple risk heartbreak if the local authority is unsuccessful in their application for a full care order, but if Sarah becomes available for adoption,

25

she'll be settled in a permanent home much sooner than is usual.

I have to wait a moment for the constriction in my chest to ease before I manage to whisper, 'OK, that's fine.' Leaning down, I touch Sarah's warm forehead with my nose, taken aback by the speed events are taking. Ending the call, I sit listening to the sounds of Sarah's even breathing and chastise myself for not managing to put my own feelings aside.

Ten a.m. the next morning I'm sitting on a fabric-covered couch in the local authority reception with Sarah fast asleep in my arms, watching the comings and goings of council employees. Sarah's breathing is deep and regular and, as I watch her, I feel my own heartbeat slowing down.

After a few minutes Sue appears. 'We're ready for you.' She crooks her finger. Obediently I follow her down a corridor decorated with children's drawings and several posters featuring smiling children above the words, 'Could you foster?'

Sue stops outside interview room two. From inside I can hear low voices and my heart beats in my throat. Meeting prospective adopters feels almost as nerve wracking as embarking on a blind date. Preparing for the worst and clenching Sarah so tightly to me that my jagged nails dig into my palms, I'm pleasantly surprised when Sue throws the door open on a young couple in their mid-thirties. Perched nervously in seats positioned side by side, they release hands and look up, smiling widely. Most adopters are in their early forties at least and I'm pleased they're a bit younger than average. It means that they may go on to adopt again in the future. It's a comfort to think that Sarah might not be an only child.

'Kate, Paul.' Sue waves her hands through the space between us. 'This is Rosie Lewis, Sarah's foster carer.'

The couple rise in unison, both proffering their hands to shake. Shifting Sarah into my left arm I offer my right, reassured by the firmness of their grip. They meet my eyes and smile warmly. 'It's lovely to meet you,' Kate says, her eyes shining as she glances down at Sarah. I like them immediately.

'Please.' Sue gestures for us to sit down and wastes no time getting to the point. 'We went to panel this morning. It was unanimously agreed that Paul and Kate are a perfect match for Sarah. So, we'll be able to get her settled into her new home for Christmas.'

'That's wonderful news,' I hear myself say, gulping down the rising emotion in my throat. Meeting her new parents brings home the inevitability of our own little separation. 'Would you like to hold her?'

Kate sits with one leg crossed over the other, jiggling her foot. 'Oh yes,' she says, nodding vigorously and turning to smile at her husband. Their eyes burn with passion as I place their future daughter in her arms.

Paul leans over and pulls the shawl down to reveal Sarah's face. She is awake now, gazing up at the new faces with interest. Kate holds out her finger and Sarah reaches out, clasping it as she did mine on the day I first met her.

Paul's eyes fill with tears. The couple exchange glances and smile at each other. I turn away, feeling like an unwelcome intruder spying on a private moment.

'Perhaps you could tell Paul and Kate a bit more about Sarah,' Sue prompts, an unusual gentleness in her tone. 'Give them an idea of her routine and what's she's like to care for.'

'She's lovely, so lovely,' I say, embarrassed to find my voice cracking.

Sue's habitually sour, downturned expression softens. She reaches out and rubs my arm, a brisk but comforting gesture. I'm overwhelmed with gratitude at the unexpected show of sympathy.

In the days leading up to the handover I find myself talking to Sarah all the time, trying to hold back my nervousness at letting her go, knowing I'll probably continue to rock for days after she has left my arms.

The night before she is due to leave I sleep uneasily, tossing and turning. My dreams are confused and when I wake in the morning I feel the same flat sadness of the last few days but decide against trying to shrug it off. It might help me to stay calm, distanced.

When I pick Sarah up from her crib at 6:30 a.m. she is wide awake and gazing around. She catches my eye and smiles so adoringly that my stomach lurches with a long-ing to keep her. Warming some milk, I realise it's the last bottle I'll ever give her. She seems to sense this, frowning in puzzlement as she sucks. I sing through my lullaby repertoire, to give her nice memories to take to her new home.

After her bottle Emily and Jamie ask to give her a short cuddle. They both seem reserved this morning and I feel another little stab of guilt, hoping these endings don't haunt them when they're older. I remind myself that fostering has helped them to develop a strong sense of empathy and kindness.

'Good luck, Sarah,' they call out before leaving for school. Tonight I plan to take them for a pizza as a reward for being part of a fostering family. It will be good to be out; the house seems to echo with an unwelcome silence for days after a placement has ended, especially a much-loved one. Anyway, Emily and Jamie deserve the important part they play in children's lives to be acknowledged.

Forcing a bright smile as I wave the children off, I lay Sarah in her crib, watching as she slowly turns her head from side to side. Her eyes drift to the twinkling lights twisted around a miniature Christmas tree on the hearth. Transfixed, her tiny lips form the shape of an 'O'. Minutes later her tiny fingers uncurl and she drops off into a relaxed sleep, reminding me how far she's come in a short period of time. Six weeks ago she was tucked up tightly in a ball of drug-induced pain.

While she's resting I pack her memory box, filling it with items that her adoptive parents will hopefully keep safe for her. I label everything carefully, including a blanket that her birth mother was thoughtful enough to buy before she went into labour and a little pink rabbit with a rattle inside, a present from her grandmother. Little details that may mean so much to her when she's older. I've also written her a life-story book filled with photos of our family, so that she has a record of where she spent her first few weeks of life. Sitting on the floor, I allow myself a few tears as I close the lid, unable to hold back any longer.

When I open the door to Desmond half an hour later I'm sure he notices my swollen eyes, but he knows better than to mention it. It's a sight he's seen on a fair number of occasions and I'm grateful for his sensitivity. I know he will hang around when the adoptive couple have left with their new daughter, to hold my hand and congratulate me on a job well done.

'You's looking particularly dreadful this morning, Rosie,' he jokes, aware that any hint at sympathy would set me off. I hoot with laughter, the chuckle catching as a little sob at the back of my throat.

Some foster carers are able to cope with separation more easily than others. I was hoping that with time I would get better at letting go, but I'm still a work in progress as far as that's concerned. With babies I find it particularly difficult to keep my distance and not become attached, even though I know my job requires me to maintain a cool professionalism.

For the next half an hour, while we wait for the new couple to arrive, I busy myself folding Sarah's freshly washed little clothes and packing them into her new Peter Rabbit suitcase. Desmond chatters away in the background but I hardly notice what he's saying, I'm so distracted. I try not to look at him, knowing that if I meet his eye my guard will come crashing down.

With fifteen minutes to pass I sit on the sofa, Sarah in my arms. I take a few deep breaths, trying to dislodge the uncomfortable knotting sensation in my stomach. Wanting some warning before they descend, so that I can gather myself, I fix my eyes on the window, watching the part of the road I can see beyond the front garden.

Paul and Kate arrive a few minutes earlier than planned, no doubt itching to begin this next exciting phase of their lives. It seems like such a long time since I first met them, even though it was only a week earlier. With older children the handover periods tend to be much longer, but with a baby as young as Sarah it's over with quickly, with only one or two pre-planned meetings before the big day.

The atmosphere is a little forced as I fuss around offering them tea and biscuits, my breakfast churning vengefully in my stomach. Kate perches on the edge of the sofa, her mouth working at the edges. Her husband hovers in the doorway, his eyes barely leaving Sarah's peaceful face as she snoozes in her crib. They're probably desperate to get away but the formalities have to be attended to, medical information imparted, etc. I try to keep the atmosphere light; this is, after all, one of the happiest days of their lives. I have heard that adopters find the final handover day almost as traumatic as the foster carer, as if they're stealing someone's own child.

With details exchanged and forms signed there is not much else to be said. Unexpectedly, Kate walks over and squeezes my arm. 'I want you to know we've waited a long time for this day. Thank you for taking such good care of her.'

The well of tears I was fighting to hold down threatens to overflow. Reassured that Sarah is going to someone sensitive and kind, I gulp, nodding in acknowledgement. I don't really trust myself to speak as I lift the sleepy baby from her crib, tucking her blanket gently around her.

'Well, tha' seems to be everything covered,' Desmond says as he walks over to me, tactfully touching my shoulder to remind me that we have a job to do.

Surrendering someone so vulnerable to an unknown future feels unnatural, wrong even. Every instinct shouts at me to hold on to Sarah but I summon all my mental energy and brush a brief kiss on her warm forehead. 'Be happy,' I whisper, ignoring the ache in my chest and planting her firmly in the social worker's arms.

As Desmond turns to cross the room I hold onto the thought that whatever life holds in store for Sarah, at least during her first six weeks she was cocooned, suspended for a short while in a net of love and safety. I hope that I'll see her again one day, even though I know it's unlikely. Adoptive couples often prefer to draw a line under the past, a sentiment I can sympathise with, however difficult it can be for foster carers to accept.

'Do you think she'll be alright?' I ask Desmond as we watch her for-ever parents settle Sarah's seat into their car then exchange a tender kiss over the open passenger door. I give up trying to hold back the tears.

Helpless

'She is a much-wanted child.' Desmond, a rock at times like this, wraps a steady arm around my trembling shoulders and draws me back into the house. 'They'll cherish her,' he assures me, leading me into the kitchen. 'You's no' to worry. Now, put tha' kettle on. I need to give you the heads up on an urgent case we've just had in.'

And so the wheel turns, I think, as I never cease to wonder how lucky I am to have found such a special job.

ROSIE LEWIS

A Small Boy's Cry

A True
Short Story

A Small Boy's Cry

With the familiar pips of the *BBC News at Ten*'s closing music pulsing away in the background, I secure the dead bolt on the back door and walk back through the kitchen. My eyes stray to the smiley face etched onto one of the cupboard doors – a legacy of three-year-old Alfie – then I go through to our 'lived-in' lounge, where a carefully placed coffee table fails to conceal a lingering pink glow on the carpet: fuchsia nail varnish, courtesy of Amy.

Amy was fifteen years old when she arrived as an emergency placement the previous year, staying with us for four weeks. By the time she left we were more or less buddies (what's a few cracked vases and a broken television between friends?), although her arrival and the ensuing days while she acclimatised to the sobering reality of living in a canna-bis-free house were, to use social services' mild description, 'challenging'.

But I don't mind that much if our home is less than perfect. Not really. Dimming the lights on our weathered but cosy rooms, I climb the stairs knowing that I wouldn't have it any other way. Smudges on the window panes or scribbles on walls can be erased with some elbow grease or a splash of paint, the effort more than compensated for by the hope that the children we have fostered aren't the only ones to leave their mark behind.

It's nice to think that the time they've spent in our family leaves its own impression. Muddy walks in windswept woodlands, splashing through puddles on a rainy afternoon, drinking hot cocoa while playing board games in front of the log fire; the simple, gentle monotony of everyday life spent with people who care leaves an imprint, perhaps even replacing some earlier, less tranquil memories. Sometimes, all it takes to make a positive difference to a young life is just one adult who cares enough to show an interest. Carving a place in a troubled heart nurtures resilience, buffering whatever turbulence may lie ahead when the haven of foster care has ended.

Up in my bedroom I climb into bed, leaving my clothes and mobile phone within reach. Tonight I'm on call and covering the eleven-to-eighteen age range, as well as my usual under-tens. Switching my electric blanket on, I can't help but wonder if I'll be needed and who it might be. When covering such a wide age range, I have to be prepared for anything. Jenny, a fostering friend of mine, recently accepted an unaccompanied minor while on call. When the Somalian arrived at her house, she couldn't help but notice his emerging facial hair and rippling six pack; it turns out that Nafiso was, in fact, twenty-one.

However much my imagination strayed, I must have dropped off fairly quickly because when my phone dances impatiently around the top of my bedside cabinet and I reach out to switch the lamp back on, the bulb is still hot. Still half asleep, I reluctantly grope for the ANSWER button.

'Hello,' I answer croakily, switching to loudspeaker mode and blinking rapidly in the soft light. My pulse quickens at the sound of Des's Scottish burr.

'I'm just giving you the heads-up, Rosie,' my supervising social worker tells me in an urgent tone, converting my adrenaline into action.

I force myself to my feet and dress hurriedly, pulling on an old jumper, leggings and a pair of fluffy socks. At 1 a.m. in mid-November, the temperature is already dipping close to zero.

'Boy, aged three. Suspected neglect. He's receiving emergency treatment at the moment. Not sure how long he'll be at the hospital but you's best get yourself ready.'

Aw, three, I think, aware of a familiar clawing in my stomach; it's the desire to make him all better before he's even arrived. Des promises to ping the details through to me and reminds me I can call him for support any time, day or night. After making a quick coffee I switch on the computer and open the email sitting in my inbox from Des.

EMERGENCY PLACEMENT REQUIRED
Charlie SMITH, age three
Charlie has been on the vulnerable children's register
since birth, as his mother, Tracy, has struggled for
years with depression and addiction issues. With
support, Tracy has demonstrated that she's able to
meet Charlie's basic needs, but he's rarely present at
nursery, and neighbours have complained of continued
bouts of crying coming from their flat. Tracy has no
extended family or network of friends to offer support.

Late this evening Charlie was found wandering the
concrete walkway below the family home. Though his
vocabulary seems limited, the boy indicated to a
passer-by that he had fallen from the first-floor
window. Police were unable to rouse his mother when
they entered the flat. She appeared to be heavily
intoxicated. Charlie's currently in A&E where he's
receiving treatment for a gash to the head. An urgent
foster placement is required while investigations are
carried out.

I click 'X' to close the window, and sit staring at the blank
screen for a moment. It sounds to me like both Charlie and
his mother have been living an isolated existence, with no
one but professionals around to offer support. My stomach
begins to churn, as it does whenever someone new is about
to arrive.

Stop fretting, I tell myself. If Des were here he would
say, 'You's haven't done too badly so far, m'darling.' All of

the children I've cared for in my years as a foster carer have left happier than when they came, so I suppose he'd be right. Knowing the trauma Charlie has been through, I feel the familiar tug to offer comfort intensifying. The chance comes sooner than expected. Just as I'm finishing the dregs of my coffee, the doorbell rings.

Charlie stands on the doorstep, the top of his mousy-coloured hair bathed in pale moonlight. The delicate skin above his right eye is covered with white gauze and tape, held in place by a bandage circling his head like a bandana. I can't see his face as he's staring down at his black plimsolls, but I notice how tiny he looks next to the stocky police officer beside him. It's freezing, but all he's wearing is a pair of dirty pyjamas. A middle-aged woman, presumably the duty social worker, hovers behind.

'I'm Evelyn,' she says, leaning around the officer who's massaging Charlie's shoulder with meaty fingers.

'Hello, Evelyn. And you must be Charlie,' I say softly, crouching down to his level.

His eyes are barely visible under a heavy crop of wispy hair, but I can sense bewilderment there. His features are small and appealing but unusually angular for a child so young – he's much too thin. His head hangs awkwardly to one side, as if it's too heavy or uncomfortable to hold up. I feel a rush of pity.

'You look freezing. Come in, all of you.'

'He wouldn't let me carry him or wrap him in my coat,' Evelyn says, as she follows me through the hall, her fingers on Charlie's back, propelling him in. His eyes are swollen with tiredness. 'And we couldn't find anything warm for him at the flat.'

She hands me a small, grubby *Fireman Sam* rucksack. 'Here are a few of his bits, but not much, I'm afraid.'

When we reach the living room she leans towards me. 'Most of his clothes were damp, covered in all sorts. Mum was so out of it we couldn't make head or tail of what she was saying.'

'It's OK,' I say. 'I have spares.'

Turning to Charlie, I kneel beside him. He stares at me with an anxious frown.

'Don't worry, Charlie, everything will be fine. We'll find you some things to wear in the morning. I'm Rosie, by the way. You'll be staying with me for a bit. You're safe here, sweetie.'

The police officer, a man in his forties with closely cropped dark hair, smiles warmly at me, then grimaces and shakes his head, his expression saying: doesn't bear thinking about, does it?

Evelyn and the officer sit on the sofa, and Charlie sinks down on the rug in the middle of the floor, exhausted.

'I know the mum.' The social worker speaks out of the corner of her mouth like a ventriloquist, as if Charlie would be unable to hear that way. 'I was hoping she'd get a grip on things, but ...' She gives a weary sigh, shrugging her shoulders. 'Well, you know ...'

I nod. How many times had I seen it now? An over-dependence on alcohol or drugs – or both – and a child's chances of having a good day or a harrowing one spin on a penny, all determined by the chemicals pulsing through their mother's veins. It's not always beatings and bruises that signal the end of a birth family and the beginning of life in foster care, I muse. Sometimes it's a simple case of daily deterioration, the slow unravelling of a mother's ability to cope. I flick my mind back to the early days, after my daughter Emily was born.

Catapulted into a life without the reassuring structure of work, I felt isolated and lonely. Each day was seemingly endless, and the monotonous cycle of changing, feeding and rocking really got me down. If someone had told me back then that I would soon choose to spend my life caring for other people's children, I would have pronounced them deluded. Remembering how lost I felt, it doesn't take a huge stretch of the imagination to think that I too might have been unable to cope, perhaps drifting towards a crutch to numb the feelings of uselessness. I shudder at the thought, feeling a stab of pity for both mother and child.

Charlie's chin is quivering. I'm not sure whether it's with cold, fear or perhaps because his head's aching.

'When did he last have pain relief?' I ask Evelyn, while I reach behind the sofa for a small, pale-blue blanket. I drape it around his shoulders then sit quietly beside him, letting him get used to having me near. He looks sideways at me with solemn eyes and I smile, noticing that his face is dotted with fine white crusts, presumably salty deposits from anxious tears at separating from Mum.

'Just before we left the hospital, about …' Evelyn inclines her head towards the police officer.

He checks his watch, pursing his lips. 'About half an hour or so ago, I'd say.'

I nod grimly, knowing that the poor little mite is in for a rough few days. With his legs splayed and shoulders hunched over, Charlie looks like he's reached the same conclusion, as if he's lost all hope at the tender age of three. Watching as he nibbles his fingernails, tearing into the ragged skin, I'm flooded with a longing to pick him up and soothe him.

It's actually this first, unscripted half an hour or so that I find the most difficult, when I'm weighing up what the child needs, trying to read their signals. I'm getting better at it. In the early days I was overly attentive, moving awkwardly around children who probably would have preferred a little distance while they adapted to their new environment. I would fuss around, straightening toy boxes that were doing perfectly well where they were, and offering endless litres of juice and other refreshments. Experience has taught me to hold back a little.

Evelyn hands me a short report from the hospital to read. I'm pleased she's decided not to discuss everything in front of Charlie, especially once I read the contents. It seems that his short life has been peppered with regular trips to the emergency department – scalding-hot tea spilt on him when he was just three months old, stitches at the age of nine months after a falling shelf happened to catch him on the head. The depressing list goes on and suddenly Charlie's mother becomes a more shadowy figure. My sympathy wanes.

A Small Boy's Cry

It's a familiar tale. Another early childhood eroded by circumstances, leaving the vulnerable – well, Charlie at least – lost, scared and sitting alone in a heap on my rug. It will take a while for the fragments of his short life to be pieced together. With an investigation underway, nursery teachers, GPs, health visitors, everyone who has come into contact with Charlie will be interviewed and the jigsaw will eventually be pieced together. Of course, there will be gaps, ones that perhaps only his mother will ever be able to fill. The emerging picture will hopefully reveal neglect and not wilful abuse; I still struggle to come to terms with the possibility that a mother could deliberately harm her own child. However many times I hear about it, my brain just can't assimilate something that disturbing.

The rest of the hospital report matches what was summarised in Des's email and, for now, what more do I need to know? Evelyn hands me a leaflet – *Care Following a Head Injury* – reminding me of my own duty of care. Every parent knows how heavily the responsibility of caring for a child can sometimes weigh, especially when they're unwell. That responsibility increases tenfold when that child is a ward of the state. For a brief moment I feel overwhelmed, but then I remind myself that help is just a phone call away, should Charlie take a turn for the worse.

'They've assured us that there's no sign of serious injury,' Evelyn says, perhaps noticing the cloud passing over my face, 'but best keep a close eye on him. It seems he had a soft landing so they don't think he bumped his head. From what the neighbours had to say, he cut his head on the lid of a tin can, but if there's any vomiting or you're at all concerned …' She makes an L shape with her forefinger and thumb, raising her hand to her ear in imitation of a phone.

'Don't worry, I'll stay close by.'

Evelyn hands me a placement agreement to sign and I scribble my signature, longing for her and the constable to leave so that I can get Charlie settled.

'Well, we'll leave you to it.'

Evelyn zips up her bag and rises to her feet. The movement rouses Charlie, who was beginning to nod off where he sat. His head shoots up and he howls, rocking back and forth in a self-soothing action. To see such a small boy surrounded by adults and yet too afraid to reach out to any of us for comfort almost makes me weep. He must think the world an unfriendly place and I wonder how he'll cope with all the turmoil ahead. Children in care have to adjust to lots of different people coming and going in their lives.

'Aw, it's all right, sweetie,' I whisper, reaching down to lift him up. His legs dangle lifelessly around my hips but he stops howling, tears rolling silently down his cheeks. He must have feared we were all about to abandon him.

'I'm not going anywhere, honey. I'm going to take care of you.'

He nuzzles his face into my shoulder. I can feel heat from his little body pressing against my side. His bandaged head rests against my cheek, the sticky tape cold against my skin. With Charlie perched on my hip I walk quickly through the hall to show Evelyn and the officer to the door, wondering if Charlie's path had been mapped out from the moment he was born. Could his mother, on the day she first cupped his tiny head in the palm of her hand, ever have imagined that barely three years later she would lose him, at least for the foreseeable future? The might of social services rides like a steam roller over families, whose fate sometimes turns on which social worker is assigned to work on their case.

On my way back to the living room I fall into the classic words of comfort – 'There, there, it's all right, you're safe here, baby, no need to cry. Hush now, sweetie, everything's going to be fine' – but I suspect that Charlie's in a place where words won't reach him. With his face tear-streaked he glances up at me, his dirty, overlong fringe falling across his eyes. Close up he smells of hospitals, although antiseptic masks another, acrid stench: tobacco and something muskier.

'Come on, sweetie. Let's get you a drink and then we'll tuck you up, shall we?'

I walk to the kitchen, chatting in soft, sing-song tones. As I pour the milk I notice him watching me with a sullen wariness. He really could do with a bath, but I won't put him through the trauma at this time of night. What he needs, over and above anything else, is sleep. I hand him a beaker of milk and he takes it, listlessly running the sippy lid over his lips.

'There's a good boy. Have a nice drink.'

He begins to cry again and I feel a familiar sharp pang in my stomach, a longing to reassure him that what he's known is not all that there is.

Ten minutes later, talking in a loud whisper so as not to wake the others, I hold his hand and guide him, still hiccoughing with tiny sobs, into the spare room.

'I want Mummy!' he wails suddenly, the sight of an unfamiliar bed filling his voice with urgency. He sinks to the floor, tears streaming down his puffy red cheeks.

Searching through the rucksack that Evelyn gave me, I try to find a comforter, something familiar that might smell of his mother and console him. Apart from a few ragged items of clothing there's nothing; no teddy or special blanket. Reaching up to the top shelf of our bookcase, I grab the first teddy I lay my hands on. Lowering my chin to my chest, I deepen my voice and make teddy pretend-talk.

'Hello, Charlie. I'm Harold. Can I come to bed with you?'

Charlie stops mid-sob, his eyebrows slowly rising with interest. Holding his breath, he stares at 'Harold' and nods, clasping the stuffed toy to his chest and wiping his tears on the soft fur. Gently steering him to bed, I half lift, half guide him in. He winces in pain as his head touches the pillow. The tears return as I switch off the main light and plug in a night lamp.

'Night, night, Charlie,' I whisper, sitting beside his bed and stroking his hair. Eventually his breathing settles and his eyes flutter to a close.

That night I stage a vigil beside his bed, setting my alarm at two-hourly intervals so that I can keep a regular eye on him. I am surprised to find that he sleeps through it all, and

I even manage to get snatches of uninterrupted sleep myself between checks. I guess that he must have been too exhausted from all the drama to fret about his unfamiliar surroundings.

At 5 a.m. I am confident enough to leave him and chance an hour's rest in my own bed. It's Saturday morning and there aren't any football matches or clubs to get the older children up for, although at just gone six o'clock I get up anyway to make sure Charlie's not lying awake and fretting. Creeping along the hall, I peer around his bedroom door – he's curled up on his side in a tight ball, one hand tucked between the pillow and his pink cheek, the other arm resting heavily on teddy. Soft dimples of flesh emerge from the cuffs of his over-small pyjamas, his tiny fingers lightly brushing against his chin. He looks angelic and, I'm relieved to find, quite relaxed.

I quietly back away and suck a lungful of fresh air from the hall; his room was redolent with the same musky smell I noticed on him last night. Before I reach the stairs there's a loud wail. Back in his room I find him sitting bolt upright in the bed, staring around in shock. He looks terrified.

'It's all right, sweetie. You're in Rosie's house.'

I crouch down beside his bed and stroke the back of his head. In daylight I can see that his eyes, though red-rimmed and fearful, are a beautiful blue-grey. He really is a gorgeous child.

'You're going to be staying with me for a little while. Do you remember me tucking you in last night?'

He gives a slight nod, hesitantly trusting.

'Where's Mummy?' he asks, his voice quavering.

'Mummy isn't feeling well at the moment but you'll see her soon, don't you worry.'

I expect more tears but he surprises me by throwing the duvet back and shuffling his bottom to the edge of the mattress.

'Me need breakfast.'

'Oh, yes, OK, sweetie, but first you need a bath.' He really does smell awful.

As I help him out of his pyjamas I have to suppress a gasp. Charlie's covered in a series of sores, all the way down his back, arms and legs. I hope I'm wrong but the small red bumps look to me like bed-bug bites. My heart sinks. If any have travelled with him in the creases of his rucksack or on his pyjamas, I'll be lucky not to have my own infestation soon.

He continues to plead for food as I lift him into the tub so I hurry things along, giving the hair at the nape of his neck a quick wash, careful not to dislodge the bandage. Not wasting time with soap, I use the shampoo suds to clean the rest of him.

As I wrap him in a towel, trying not to rub the sores, I hear movement in the corridor. Charlie's widened eyes tell me he's noticed, too.

'It's all right, honey. That's the other children getting up. We'll just brush your teeth, and then we'll go and meet them, shall we?'

His chest puffs out and his big eyes blink, tears brimming. Reaching into the cupboard for a new, toddler-sized toothbrush I tell him, 'They're lovely children. They'll be very pleased you're here.'

Charlie stares at the toothbrush in amazement. Every time I put it in his mouth he pulls away and grabs my hand, twisting and turning the alien object so he can examine it from every angle. When I finally get a good look at his teeth I realise that he's probably never owned his own toothbrush or even used one before; they're all chipped and grey, his gums so inflamed that after just a few seconds of brushing his saliva is streaked with blood. When he swills water and spits into the sink I break into song to distract him. 'The wheels on the bus go round and round ...' He's already upset. I don't want the gory contents spinning down the plughole to completely freak him out.

Charlie frowns, watching me with suspicion. 'That stick maked blood come,' he says accusingly, pointing at the toothbrush.

'Never mind, you're fine,' I say, steering him briskly away and stowing the toothbrush in a holder of its own. Without knowing Charlie's full history, I have to bear in mind that he could be incubating a blood-borne infection like hepatitis or even HIV. He follows me out of the bathroom, Harold clutched tightly in his hand.

'Aw, look at him. He's so cute!' my daughter Emily exclaims, her brother Jamie already on his knees, pulling faces and trying to elicit a laugh. Phoebe, a nine-year-old girl who has lived with us for eight months, stands behind them, staring at the new arrival with concern. Suspecting she's worried that he might usurp her position I slip my arm around her, squeezing her shoulder.

'Charlie, here's Phoebe, and this is Jamie and Emily. I'm sure they'd love to be friends with you, wouldn't you, guys?'

'Yes, course. You'll love it here, Charlie,' Jamie tells him in a soothing tone.

Emily nods and pats him on the arm. Phoebe copies Emily by nodding but she still looks dubious. Charlie stares at everyone, visibly shrinking away. Instinctively, Emily knows how to put him at ease. She reaches for Harold, balances the soft toy on her head, and sneezes loudly. Harold rolls off and lands in Charlie's lap. I was worried the sudden noise might startle him but his face breaks into a large grin, and then quickly grows serious again.

'Me need break-f-a-s-t,' he reminds me, his voice rising with anxiety.

It's not unusual for children in care to have food issues. Many come from an environment where regular meals are unheard of and they survive by grazing on what they can find lurking at the back of a cupboard, although when Phoebe first arrived it was the opposite problem: she ate nothing but a few spoonfuls of porridge.

Charlie's mother being a drug user, it figures that food would probably appear low on her list of necessary weekly purchases.

'Yes, me too, Mum. What's for breakfast?' Jamie asks.

I should have told Charlie not to worry; Jamie would never allow me to forget a mealtime. My son is going through a growth spurt and food is an obsession second only to cricket.

'Come on, then. Let's go and make some pancakes.'

I reach out to Charlie and he stands up, slipping his small hand into mine. Jamie, Emily and Phoebe charge downstairs, the sudden withdrawal of attention pricking Charlie's interest. When we get downstairs he follows them with his eyes, watching their every move as I whip up the pancake mixture. At the table he wolfs down his food, all the while studying them closely. Whenever they look at him he quickly turns away.

We spend the whole day at home, giving Charlie time to get used to his immediate surroundings before exposing him to the world outside. Emily and Jamie revel in having a little one to play with again, enthusiastically pulling toys from the cupboard and parading them in front of him. He comes to life and for the most part he seems to enjoy their company, but he's easily distracted, spinning around at the slightest background noise. I suspect that he's watching out for danger, which speaks volumes in terms of his past experiences.

Throughout the day Charlie tumbles casually onto my lap for regular hugs, pushing himself against my back as if he'll only achieve the reassurance he craves by tucking himself beneath my skin. I have to acclimatise myself to being pawed all day – Emily and Jamie drape an arm around me occasionally or slouch next to me on the sofa, but I'm redundant as far as earthy demands for close contact go. I'd almost forgotten how exhausting it is to be needed so intensely; by teatime I'm craving the solace of my duvet, counting the hours until I can retreat to my bedroom alone.

On Sunday morning I set my alarm early again, wanting to be nearby when Charlie wakes up. Yawning, I peer around his bedroom door and suddenly all trace of tiredness evaporates, my eyes widening in terror. He's gone. Stumbling into his room, I tear back the duvet and rummage around the empty sheet, as if doing so might conjure his reappearance.

My rational head tells me not to panic – all the exterior doors are locked so he can't have gone far. But then the news story of the incident where a toddler climbed into a washing machine during a game of hide and seek, closing the door on himself, flashes into my mind. A search party found the two-year-old suffocated.

With a montage of disastrous scenarios unspooling before my eyes I shriek out his name, tearing back downstairs to check the washing machine, tumble dryer, even the fridge.

'What's going on, Mum?' Emily, Jamie and Phoebe charge bleary-eyed into the kitchen. 'What's wrong?'

Squinting, I notice another pair of bare feet behind Phoebe's. I let out a long breath.

'Charlie, where were you, honey?'

I kneel in front of him and stroke his long hair back from his forehead, unconsciously performing a quick health check.

Charlie points innocently at Phoebe, whose smile is rapidly evaporating.

'He was in my room. We were only playing,' she says, simultaneously defensive and hurt.

'You mustn't play together in the bedrooms, you know that.'

Phoebe looks suddenly crestfallen and I realise that, still recovering from the shock of seeing his bed empty, my tone must have been sharp. Until recently, Phoebe had no idea how to play with other children. It's lovely that she's chosen to share her toys with Charlie of her own accord.

'It's all right, honey. I'm sorry, it's my fault. I should have reminded you of the rules. I think it's very kind of you to be so welcoming to Charlie. How about we bring some of your toys down to show him?'

'Yay!' Phoebe cheers, and runs back to her room.

Charlie claps his hands and scrambles onto the sofa, all trace of yesterday's shyness gone. The resilience of children never fails to surprise me.

'Me be good boy,' he announces, bouncing up and down on the cushions in spite of his injured head.

I'm about to tell him that the sofa is for sitting on when Phoebe arrives back in the living room, armed with piles of toys. Charlie's eyes light up and he throws himself down on the sofa on his tummy, then rolls to the floor.

'Be careful of your head, Charlie,' I say, cringing, but his kamikaze antics don't seem to have caused him any pain.

Emily and Jamie, well past playing with toys at their age, join in eagerly now they have a young housemate to entertain. I go off to the kitchen to prepare breakfast, the sound of their loud laughter bringing a smile to my face.

Sometimes, when we welcome a child into our family, relationships are thrown out of kilter. It can take a while to establish a new fulcrum, but with younger ones it's much easier to rearrange ourselves around them, perhaps because it feels more natural for older ones to make way for the new.

With breakfast on the table, the three older children take their places; Jamie, unsurprisingly, the first to sit down.

'Come on, Charlie. Breakfast time,' I say.

Knowing how desperate Charlie was to eat yesterday, I can hardly believe that he rejects the invitation with barely a glance, continuing to play with Phoebe's toys.

'Come on, honey.' I slip my hands under his arms and try to lift him to his feet, but he arches his back then suddenly plays dead, taking advantage of my surprise by wriggling free. I lunge for him a couple of times but he dodges me, screeching in triumph. I suppose I should feel encouraged, knowing that he would only strop if feeling safe and secure. Part of me feels pleased. The rest of me is weary.

'Guess what I've got over here,' Jamie says, his tone enticing.

Charlie's head shoots around, so I go and take my place at the table, leaving my son to work the magic therapy that seems to come so easily to children.

'I think Charlie's going to like this, Mum,' Jamie says, lowering his voice theatrically.

It's one of his strengths, the art of persuasion. I'm convinced that my son has the makings of a future MP. The beginning of a smile touches Charlie's lips and he crawls slowly to the table, kneeling up when he reaches Jamie's chair.

'Me see?'

Jamie shakes his head. 'Sit up first, then I'll show you.' I could have hugged him.

Charlie performs a convoluted roll onto his tummy then rises on all fours, drawing the whole process out as long as he can. Standing, he plants such a small part of his bottom on the chair that he has to grip hold of the edge of the table for balance. He looks at me, a glint of defiance still lurking in his eyes. I lean back in my chair and stretch, heading off a battle of wills by looking casual and faking a yawn.

'Me see now?'

'OK,' Jamie announces, strumming a drum beat on the table. 'Are you ready? Ta-da!' he shouts, producing a banana.

Expecting Charlie's face to fall with disappointment I prepare to grab him before he slips off his seat, but I'm surprised to find that his eyes widen in amazement.

'S'dat?' he asks, pointing.

'It's a banana, of course. That's so obvious,' Phoebe says, tutting and rolling her eyes.

Jamie peels the fruit, looking at me.

'Can he have some, Mum?'

'Yes, of course.'

Charlie sticks his finger into the fruit and it breaks in half. He picks it up and turns it over several times in his hands, looking at it with the same interest that he showed in the toothbrush. Emily, realising the significance, cocks her head on her shoulder, her eyes brimming with tears.

'Ah, bless him, Mum,' she says quietly, looking towards me. 'I don't think he's ever seen a banana before.'

Since Charlie had been removed from home suddenly, contact with his mother is arranged at the earliest opportunity. Tracy Smith was offered a session at 9 a.m. but she declined, pronouncing early mornings 'difficult'. And so at a few minutes before 11 a.m. on Monday morning I walk into the contact centre with Charlie pottering along behind, so close that the soles of my feet brush his little legs with every stride. Knowing how much reassurance Charlie craves, I desperately hope that the meeting will go well.

The receptionist smiles a welcome and tells me that Tracy is waiting for us in the Oak suite, one of the contact rooms. I tense as we pass through a large waiting area; liaising with birth parents can be tricky. Emotions, understandably, run high and sometimes foster carers bear the brunt of it.

We pass a thin woman in her early thirties sitting on a dark-blue sofa. My attention is drawn to her because she's wearing flip-flops, even though it's November. She stares blankly at the wall ahead and I can't help but notice that her eyes are glazed over with the vacant look of a toddler watching television on a loop.

Scanning the wall opposite, I can't work out what she's so transfixed by. It's bare, barring a few scratches in the paintwork and other, more dubious-looking splotches. It looks like someone has been preparing to redecorate. Apart from traces of old Blu-tack, there's no sign of the posters that usually feature in contact centres – 'Are You Claiming All You're Entitled to?' or 'Domestic Violence Is a Crime, Report It.'

As we near the Oak suite, Charlie runs two or three feet ahead, enticed by the sight of unfamiliar toys. I find myself absent-mindedly imagining the posters that might feature in less impoverished areas, perhaps 'Trouble Finding Suitable Stables? Have You Considered Pony Sharing?' or 'Inheritance Tax a Burden? Call Us for Independent Financial Advice'. It's only when I catch up with Charlie and see that no one else is in the playroom that I stop mid-step, some inbuilt facial-recognition program finally kicking into gear. Charlie's already mounting a rather sickly looking rocking horse and so I leave him where he is, walking backwards from the room so that I can still keep my eye on him but check out the woman on the sofa. There's definitely a family resemblance.

'Excuse me,' I call out, hovering midway between the playroom and the waiting area. 'Are you Charlie's mother?'

There's a prolonged pause before she turns around, as if she's a news reporter communicating via a temperamental satellite link. Eventually she nods and stands, unsmiling, staring as she walks towards me with the same unswerving attention that she gave the blank wall. She carefully negotiates every step and as she approaches I realise why she looks like she's being operated by remote control; she smells strongly of alcohol and cigarettes. Her pale blonde hair is greasy and so is her face, like she's coated in some sort of filmy substance. She's wearing a short denim skirt and her thin legs, not surprisingly considering the weather, are mottled by the cold.

My hand flickers at my side as she nears, as I wonder whether to offer a handshake. Tracy resolves my indecision by walking past me, straight into the playroom.

'There you are, Charlie. Wha'd'ya go walking right past me for?'

Charlie swings around to the door, slipping off the horse and landing awkwardly on his bottom. He whimpers and cradles his head but it's me he looks to for reassurance, even though his mother is standing closer to him. Already we share an unspoken understanding. After such a short time I am his 'safe base', his source of protection and comfort; yet another serious cause for concern. I smile with a sympathetic glance but don't do anything more; experience has taught me that nothing winds mothers up more ferociously than taking over and playing mum in their presence.

It's only then that Tracy acknowledges me, giving a curt nod.

'I'm Rosie,' I say, smiling, willing her to scoop Charlie up.

She doesn't. Bending over, she knocks his shoulder with the back of her hand. Accidentally? With affection? It's difficult to tell, but what's obvious is that Charlie's now hyper-alert; if he were a kitten his back would be arched, his fur up on end. His bottom lip quivers. The sympathy I feel for him swells to fill up my chest and I feel irritated with myself for ever feeling any for her.

Rotating on his bottom, Charlie follows her around the room with his eyes. Instead of sitting beside him on the floor as I had hoped, she sits on one of the straight-backed chairs at the rear of the room and reaches into her handbag for her phone.

Charlie continues to study her, his brow furrowed. Is he looking for clues as to her mood? I wonder. There are a hundred questions in that little stare, one of which is perhaps, 'Why?' Tracy's bland expression must signal safety on this occasion because he potters over to her, resting a small but slightly hesitant hand on her knee.

'I've 'at to get two buses to get here, and they haven't given me no fare money yet,' she moans, lips tight with bitterness.

I hesitate, not sure how to respond. Does she expect me to commiserate?

'How tiring,' I manage to say, couching my words in an overly polite tone.

Take a look at your son, I want to say. He looks so alone. I find myself eager for contact to come to an end so I can draw him into a cuddle. It won't be the same, it won't mean as much, but it might go some way towards soothing that furrowed brow. Does she not know that it's her job to show him how lovable he is?

Before I became a foster carer I'd never considered that the ability to accept love was a skill that needed to be learned. I'd imagined that every child exits the womb with an innate capacity to be cherished. Tracy, surly and hostile, yet curiously frail, looks like she's never had an affectionate cuddle in her life. I suppose it shouldn't be surprising that she can't pass a gift on to her son that she herself was never given in the first place. Remembering how ferociously Charlie clung to me as I put him to bed last night I can't help but feel terribly sad, knowing that he had to come to a stranger to get some affection.

Out of nowhere Charlie lunges at Tracy, scratching her face. She gasps and clamps her hand to her cheek, the other bunching into a fist.

'You f*cking bully!' she screams, looking ready to shake him. Her eyes dart from him to me, weighing up whether she can get away with giving him a quick slap. 'See what he did to me?'

It was glaringly obvious that Charlie lashed out in desperation for some sort of attention. Negative or not, anything was better than indifference.

'He's a little animal. Like yer f*cking dad, you are.'

He learned at your feet, I feel tempted to say. Instead I stay silent, making a conscious effort to loosen my tightened jaw. Since fostering I've battled to master my renegade expressions, but by the look of suspicion on Tracy's face my success is questionable.

The awkward moment passes when her mobile goes off.

'Hello,' she says, brushing Charlie aside and resting her crusted feet on a large yellow tipper truck. For the next half an hour she receives a number of different calls while I play with her son, each conversation peppered with swear words. I like to think I'm not a prude – actually, remembering some of the conversations I've had with the likes of Amy and other teens, I know I'm not – but I can't help bristling at the vulgarity of this woman. The most attention Charlie gets from her is when she hangs up on someone called Dwayne and holds up her phone to take a picture of him.

'Photos aren't allowed during contact, I'm afraid,' I tell her.

Tracy's face reddens as she rises and, sensing an ill wind, I steer Charlie towards a wooden garage and a box of cars, hoping he'll become absorbed. Her feet slap slap towards me and she stops barely a foot away.

'You telling me I can't take photos of my own kid? Why don't you go f*ck yourself?'

This close up I notice that her eyes are the same blue-grey as Charlie's, except the whites of hers are threaded with the tracks of broken capillaries. For a split second I glimpse symmetry with her son; in the angle of her lips and the curve of her cheeks. With their faces momentarily merged into one, Tracy seems suddenly familiar and the connection warms me to her. For the first time I'm able to see past the hostility, registering the sense of hopelessness reflected in her dull, tired eyes. I can't help but wish there was something I could do to help.

'I'm sorry. I don't make the rules.'

She furrows her brow, wrong-footed by my conciliatory tone. For a brief moment she looks like she can't decide whether to hit me or fall into my arms for a hug.

'What's all that over 'is hands?' she asks, regaining her composure and striding across the room to Charlie.

She yanks his arm towards her and he looks up, startled. This is familiar territory – a mother desperate to minimise her own guilt by finding something to criticise in another woman's care, as if mucky hands are negligence on a par with falling from a first-floor window.

'It's felt-tip pen,' I say soothingly, trying to calm her so she'll release her hold on his arm. He looks terrified.

'He had a lovely time drawing you a picture. I have it here, actually,' I say, trying to deflect her attention and digging deep to draw on some humility. However difficult, it's in everyone's interests for foster carers to build positive relationships with birth parents.

'Would you like to show Mummy what you made for her, Charlie?'

Charlie scampers after me as I rustle around in my bag. When she sees the picture her face softens, breaking into what I imagine to be a rare smile. With an inward wince I realise why Charlie was so surprised to see a toothbrush; spear-like teeth jut from Tracy's swollen gums at such awkward angles that I imagine it must be uncomfortable for her even to talk, let alone eat. I feel an unconscious rush of genuine compassion.

'Aw, thanks. I like that, mate,' she says.

His thin chest expands and, beaming up at her, he throws his short arms around one of her legs. She briefly pats him on the back then begins pacing the room in tight circles, her fingers working over the keys of her mobile phone with such diligence it's as though she's being paid to produce a certain number of words per minute.

Charlie looks as if someone has taken a pin and stuck it in his chest. Deflated, he turns his attention back to me, sombrely offering me toys to pass comment on. I exclaim animatedly as I take each one, trying to rouse a smile. It works, although every now and again he glances around, staring at his mother with a yearning that breaks my heart. An hour and a half after we first arrived, when I tell her that contact is coming to an end, Tracy buries her face in her sleeve and sniffs loudly. Charlie's face clouds with confusion, then he joins her, tears rolling down his cheeks. I feel the familiar prickle of my own empathetic tears threatening to spill over. She's a mother, after all, and one who can probably taste the fear of losing a part of her forever. I can't imagine that any woman would ever truly want that.

Later that afternoon Emily, Jamie and Phoebe decide to watch a DVD. Unable to agree on one, Emily and Jamie begin to tussle, each grabbing their own disc and trying to reach the DVD player before the other. It's a playful exchange and I can tell that Phoebe wants to join in, but horseplay with foster children is forbidden.

'Come on, you two,' I say, not wanting the others to feel left out. 'That's enough.'

Ready to launch herself into the scrum, Phoebe looks disappointed. What I hadn't noticed in all of this was Charlie's reaction. He's crouching in the corner of the room, shuddering with fright. As I approach him he throws his head back, screaming in terror. His arms are locked at the elbows, his legs stiff with fear. As I crouch and take him into my arms his body is rigid, trembling and sweaty. Rocking, I murmur reassurance and eventually he relaxes, nuzzling close.

Phoebe approaches and kneels silently in front of us. Her brow furrows, perhaps remembering how frightened she was when she first came to us. Reaching out, she touches his face with the edge of one finger and softly strokes his cheek. She's come a long way from the detached, troubled girl who arrived so many months ago. I'm so touched by her gentleness that I have to look away to gather myself. Charlie gives us both a watery smile.

Over the next few days I keep replaying the build-up to Charlie's panic attack, trying to pinpoint the trigger. The only conclusion I come to is that a simple play-fight ignited the memory of a much more traumatic event. I find not knowing exactly what he may have gone through disturbing but wonder whether, at his tender age, he even possesses the words to tell anyone.

As is sometimes the way, synchronicity helps things along a little, a chance meeting barely two days later shedding some light on his past. It's Charlie's second weekend with us and on Sunday morning, bundled up in coats, scarves and hats, we set off for a walk to our local park. Nestled between Emily and Phoebe, Charlie holds their hands and bounds along, chanting their names. Every so often he's rewarded with a swing high in the air. Whooping with glee, he shouts, 'More! 'Gain!' Apart from bedtimes when he still asks, 'Where's Mummy?' he seems to have settled amazingly well into our family, revelling in the attention that comes with being the youngest member.

After feeding the ducks we walk along the river, trying to decide which of the little cafés to pop into for a hot-chocolate treat.

And that's when it happens.

With the café identified, Emily, Jamie and Phoebe quicken their step but Charlie stops abruptly as if he's walked into a lamppost, standing stock still in front of me. I rest my gloved hands on his shoulders and lean over the top of his head.

'Come on, Char—' I begin to say, but the words freeze on my lips when I catch sight of his expression. His eyes are wide and staring at a point to the right, so fixated that even when I kneel in front of him, grasp his upper arms and gently sway him to and fro, I can't get him to look at me.

Glancing over my shoulder, I try to follow his line of sight. In front of us a young mother, her hair fixed in a ponytail, is leaning over a pram, tucking a fluffy blanket around an unseen infant. Slightly ahead of her is the heavy form of a scruffy man dressed in a tracksuit top and jeans. As I turn slowly back to face Charlie a cold prickle creeps across my scalp so that the roots of my hair tingle.

'Do you know that man, Charlie?' I ask.

Charlie's holding his breath but he manages a stiff nod.

'Who is he, sweetie?' I ask gently, half tempted to follow the footsteps rapidly receding along the towpath.

Charlie begins to wail, the noise so primal that Emily, Phoebe and Jamie are back at my side within seconds, shock evident on their faces. The four of us surround Charlie and, cushioned, he begins to calm down.

For the rest of the day Charlie is withdrawn and unusually tired. I prepare his bath straight after dinner and when he's all wrapped up in his towel I hold him on my lap for a bit longer than usual. Kissing his sweet-smelling hair, I find myself wishing I could see the thoughts that swirl around his mind. After a bedtime story I leave him in his room to flick through a picture book while I fetch him a drink.

Back upstairs minutes later, armed with a glass of warm milk and a biscuit, I walk into Charlie's room to find his bed stripped and no sign of him anywhere.

'Where are you, cheeky?' I call out, drawn to the bathroom by a ruffling noise.

I pull up short in the doorway, surprised to see him tucked up in the tub, covered with his duvet and resting his head on a pillow.

'You cheeky monkey!' I shriek, but the look of seriousness on his face instantly tells me that this is not a case of toddler antics. Crouching beside him I notice that the pillow is already sodden from the residue of bubbles after his bath, the newly applied bandage curled and damp at the back of his head.

'What are you doing in there, sweetie?'

'I tometimes sleeped in the bath,' he says, his lower lip quivering with cold.

'In the bath? Why?'

'Betoz I can't heared the man fighting Mummy when I slept in the bath.'

I gulp, a wave of pity washing over me.

'The man we saw today?'

He nods, his eyes wide and searching.

'Don't you ever sleeped in the bath, Wosie?'

I shake my head, blinking rapidly.

'No, sweetie,' I smile, and stroke his hair. 'I would find it a bit too hard.'

It takes a while to persuade Charlie back into his own room and several promises that 'nasty men are not allowed in Rosie's house'.

When I go to bed I can't shake the image of Charlie's thin body shivering as he chases sleep in a makeshift porcelain bed. Before fostering I was shielded from the harshness that goes on behind closed doors. As far as I was concerned, my family, with its loving patience and understanding, was a microcosm of the world. I knew bad things happened but somehow I was cocooned, impervious to them. As a foster carer I've seen the worst side of human nature: children used to satiate sick perversions; toddlers strapped in their buggies for days at a time, leaving their parents free to shoot up with abandon; babies left whimpering in damp and dirty cots instead of being cradled close.

Having seen awful things happening to the most vulnerable, my childish hope that a compassionate master stands at the helm of a harsh universe has been all but crushed. Fostering shines a light on lives far removed from my own and I sometimes think it's an insight I'd prefer not to have. But then I remind myself of all the many small kindnesses I've seen towards the children I look after, not only from my own friends, family and fellow foster carers, but also from neighbours, health professionals, even people I bump into at the supermarket – and I'm reassured that those who want to do harm are outnumbered tenfold. Besides, when I'm between placements I feel hollow; fostering fills that void with the needs of others. It's a job that defines me and so I'm drawn willingly back to the vacancy register.

Fretting about the effect the encounter by the river would have on the progress Charlie has made with us, it takes a while for me to drop off to sleep.

I needn't have worried.

The next morning Charlie runs to me with his arms outstretched. I reach out to him and clasp his hands in my own before bending my knees.

'Come on, then,' I say, with a playful sigh.

It's a little routine we've got going and he gives a roar of delight, climbing onto my knees and then making the attempt to scale my thighs. I squat a bit lower to give him some purchase and he frowns, puffing his cheeks out with exertion. When his feet reach my tummy I straighten up and whizz him round in a circle. He giggles until the breath catches in his throat, then he hooks both legs around me and hangs back so that the top of his head brushes the floor.

'Wosie, 'gain, 'gain!'

* * *

Two weeks later I pack the few clothes I've managed to buy for Charlie into a small suitcase, ready for him to move on. It's a shame that he can't stay with us; we've a vacancy but, following the recent introduction of a tiered allowances system, the local authority will save money if he's moved to a less experienced carer.

Since only experienced Level 3 carers can be placed on call, any child brought into care as an emergency – the most traumatic way to enter the system – faces another move soon afterwards. I sometimes think that social workers become desensitised to moving children on, not fully acknowledging the devastating impact that frequent moves have on a child's psyche.

Fortunately for Charlie, he's moving on to a carer who lives locally and, knowing the family he's going to, I'm confident that he'll continue to thrive. As I help him into his new coat and shoes he leans into me, reluctant to leave. Phoebe hovers behind and my heart goes out to her. She looks bereft, perhaps reflecting on her own past loss and the ones that will inevitably follow.

Emily and Jamie watch with glum faces as Charlie rests his head on my shoulder and plays with my hair. Later, I'll soothe them with the knowledge that, even if we never see Charlie again, he's woven into the fabric of our family by an invisible thread of memories. A picture of Charlie will join the montage of faces smiling out at us from our fostering album, embroidered into the tapestry of our lives and reminding us of all the many things we take for granted in our settled existence.

Epilogue

One of the most frustrating things for a foster carer is to be left wondering how a child fares when they've left the foster home, so it was nice that Charlie went to a local family that I knew. I received regular updates on his progress and about a year after he moved on from us I heard that his birth father had been identified (after testing the DNA of a number of possibles suggested by his mother).

Charlie's father had no idea of the little boy's existence and was overwhelmed but delighted by the news. Following an assessment by social services, Charlie went to live with his father and grandmother. He is now thriving, as much a gift for them as they are for him.

ROSIE LEWIS

Two More Sleeps

A True
Short Story

Two More Sleeps

Sometimes there's a fine line between fair and failing parents.

I don't envy social workers the responsibility of deciding when that threshold has been breached, especially when the lines are blurred. Before I began fostering, my mind would airbrush over shades of grey, preferring the reassuring palette of black and white. I didn't like to hear that Hitler was a disarming and humorous man of faith who nursed his mother when she was ill – the contradiction was discomforting, at odds with my blueprint of good and evil. When a documentary on the Discovery Channel claimed that the man responsible for the Holocaust was also wonderful with children, I switched the TV off in denial.

The watershed came when I met the birth mother of my second fostering placement, back in 2004. Knowing that Lauren had kept two-year-old Freddie locked in a damp room with no comfort and little to eat, my mind had conjured such a monstrous picture of her that when she turned up at my house for contact, I almost goggled in surprise. Frail and unkempt, she seemed almost as helpless as the little one she had brought into the world.

It was a defining moment, and years later, in December 2010, Lauren's simultaneous capacity for callousness and vulnerability touched my thoughts as I hurried along the high street for the third time in as many hours. I was on my way to collect Angell, a young boy who had been taken into protective custody by police earlier that day. The four-year-old had been found by a dog walker, half dressed and huddled beneath a park bench in a children's playground. With fierce blasts of air prickling my skin, it was difficult to comprehend a mother leaving her child alone and unprotected in sub-zero temperatures, but then memories of Lauren resonated in my mind. I reminded myself that, when it came to human nature, there were few certainties or absolutes.

The police station was a sturdy three-storey Victorian building, conspicuous among the shops for its lack of tinsel and festive frills, on the corner of the street. Its wide sash windows blinked beacons of cool white light into the frosty air, as if keeping watch over the town. Sidestepping an icy puddle, I climbed the stone steps towards the entrance and was almost knocked off my feet by a gangly, hooded youth who lumbered through the open door, elbows at bony right-angles, pale face puckered at the lips around a newly lit cigarette.

Two More Sleeps

The grim-faced, suited man in his wake bestowed an apologetic nod in my direction, raising his eyebrows as if to say: I can think of nicer places to spend Christmas Eve. Narrowing my eyes against the smoke, I threw him a quick, sympathetic smile in return, absently wondering whether he was a beleaguered parent, an appropriate adult enlisted to ensure fair-play in interview or perhaps even a fellow foster carer.

The heated reception area offered a welcome sanctuary from the wind and once inside I let out a sigh of relief and stamped my frozen feet, setting my duffel bag on the floor. On the other side of a glass-fronted enquiry desk several telephones demanded attention in shrill tones and a printer suddenly spluttered, coughing itself awake.

With gloved, stiffly frozen fingers I pressed the buzzer for attention then sat down on a wooden bench and waited. Soon a police constable, perhaps somewhere in her mid-forties, weaved her way between the empty desks of the front office, the radio clipped to her chest accompanying each of her steps with loud, crackling hisses. 'Sorry we messed you around earlier,' she said through the grille after checking my Bright Heights Fostering Agency security pass. 'I'm sure you could have done without all the to'ing and fro'ing, today of all days. I'm Jo, by the way.'

'I didn't mind, Jo,' I replied honestly as she joined me in reception. 'It was good to get out of the house, to tell you the truth.'

She laughed, gently nudging my upper arm with her epauletted shoulder. 'It'd do my head in being cooped up with my lot for days on end. That's why I always volunteer for the holiday shift.'

I gave her a complicit smile but, for me, it was more the distraction I was grateful for than an escape from the demands of close family. The initial call about Angell came through from my fostering agency just after lunchtime and since then I had made two aborted trips to collect him. There was lots to do at home but Sarah, a new-born baby I had looked after for six weeks, had moved into her forever home just seven days earlier and my arms were still feeling empty without her nestled there. The drama was just what I needed to stop me fretting about how well she was settling with her new parents.

Besides, I had made good use of the time. Children often come into care with only the clothes they were standing up in and so, in the last few available shopping hours, I had bought some essentials – a waterproof all-in-one coat, thick pyjamas, hat, gloves, tops and trousers – as well as some toys that I thought a four-year-old might like.

My own children, Emily and Jamie, were still busily wrapping the gifts when I left the house for the third time, their grandmother replacing the sparkly curtains in the spare room with a pair featuring Fireman Sam. 'Red tape was it?' I asked, reaching down for the duffel bag then following the officer through a security door and down a long, nondescript corridor.

'Oh no, not this time, for a change,' Jo said, throwing a wry smile over her shoulder. 'I mean, they're running a skeleton staff at social services today so it took a while to get hold of a social worker but the main issue was Mum.' Jo half-turned towards me again when she reached another door. 'She needs medical attention but she's been refusing to go anywhere without the boy.'

Adeptly, the officer punched a four-digit code into an entry system and I followed her through to another corridor, loud shouts filtering through from the floor below. Heightened yells and a clunk followed, presumably the slamming of a viewing hatch or perhaps a lock being secured. 'She's refusing to talk to us unless we agree to keep them together. The only way we could calm her down was to promise she could meet you. I hope you don't mind. She put up a real fight.'

'Of course I don't mind,' I said, shaking my head. Maternal aggression has always fascinated me: mothers turning fearless and laying down their lives if their offspring are threatened. In the words of Stephen King, 'There's no bitch on earth like a mother frightened for her kids.' Jo sounded personally affronted by what she dismissed as 'a lot of silly fuss' but I was happy to talk to Angell's mother and try to put her mind at rest. Not many parents would be comfortable with sending their child off with a total stranger.

'This whole building has been sold off. We're moving into the civic centre in the New Year and the interview rooms are loaded with confidential files so we've had to accommodate mother and child in the custody suite. Not ideal,' she said, glancing back, 'but with Mum getting a bit feisty it probably wasn't a bad idea to keep them somewhere secure.'

I was about to answer when the sound of a voice, shrill and unhinged, reached me. Jo charged ahead down a flight of metal stairs and an image popped into my head of an anguished woman, hair wild, face streaked with tears. I wondered whether the screams were coming from Angell's mother – it sounded as if she wasn't going to relinquish her child without a fight. My stomach lurched, worried about what sort of state Angell might be in. It was such a stressful situation to be plunged into. I had seen it a few times now – mothers so desperate to keep their babies that they attempted to snatch them during contact, particularly when their final, goodbye forever session loomed.

The act seemed to infuriate some of the contact supervisors. They regarded absconding as an act of selfishness but I knew that if I had found myself in that situation when Emily and Jamie were small, the lioness in me would have stirred. Most attempts fail but there have been cases where young children and even babies have gone missing from care, some never to be found again. It took me a while to realise that even neglectful or abusive mothers have a primordial instinct to hold on to their offspring.

Jo interrupted my thoughts, coming to a halt outside another heavy-looking door, this one armoured like a fortress. She turned to face me, slipping her thumbs into the top of her utility belt. A pair of handcuffs glinted silver in the artificial light. 'How much have you been told?'

'Well, not a lot really. I know he's four. I know Mum was arrested this morning for assaulting a police officer. That's about it.'

She gave a curt nod. 'Poor little bugger was scared silly. Nicki, that's Mum, turned up at the playground twenty minutes after he'd been found, claiming that he'd wandered off.' Jo signalled her scepticism by making quote marks with her fingers. 'When we told her we'd be contacting social services she kicked off big style, right in front of him. He's very timid. Been stuck here all day and we haven't heard a peep out of him yet, except for all the sobbing.'

My heart squeezed a little but Jo carried on, briskly and unmoved.

'Anyway, what can you do with them?' She asked the question with a shrug and then turned her attention back to the security pad. It struck me as a little unfair to pigeon-hole Angell's mother with all the criminals Jo had dealt with over the years, as if they were all equally culpable with no varying degrees or mitigating circumstances.

Jo swiped a security card under a flashing red laser fixed to the wall and after a series of small clicks the light turned green. Inside the custody suite there was a high counter stretching across the length of the space, punctuated at even intervals with computer terminals. Thick plastic shields were fixed to the back of each PC, presumably to protect the technology from rowdy prisoners. A heavy-set officer glanced up from behind one of the desks as I followed Jo towards a row of doors, his look of boredom giving way to one of slight surprise as I passed by.

'In here,' Jo said quietly and I took a breath as she opened one of the doors, daunted and faintly embarrassed by the unenviable task ahead. We walked into a small, nondescript room with nothing in it but a desk and two metal chairs. Surprised, I was about to turn and ask Jo where the family were when I noticed a cloudy glass partition in the wall. On the other side of the glass was a room mirroring our own, except there, sprawled on one of the chairs with her legs open, was a young woman. It was a relief to see that she was sitting placidly, her arms around the small boy on her lap. Framing her face in a drab black curtain was her hair, long, tangled and unwashed. Her eyes were heavily shadowed with dark rings, one of them swollen and red, as if she'd been punched. She seemed dazed but calm, her lips moving as if singing. Close to sleep, her son was leaning into her with his mouth slightly open, eyes flickering.

'We use this room for observing interviews,' Jo said with a tilt of her head. 'It's a one-way mirror so Mum can't see us. She's what we call a "reluctant detainee" so I just wanted to give you the heads-up on how we're going to play it if she kicks off again. You wait by the door. I'll introduce you and Mum can have a few words. Then I'll take him,' she said this with a resolute nod. 'I'll need you to leave straight away, no half measures. Any hesitation will only make things worse.'

I nodded but I was only half-listening to Jo, my chest beginning to tighten with anxiety.

'Right then,' she said and I followed her out of the room. Jo hesitated outside the next door for a fraction of a second. Rolling her shoulders back, she closed her eyes and took a little breath before bowling ahead, a telling indication of her true feelings. I felt a flash of admiration for her then: she really was quite petite, her stature incongruous with the heavy stab vest and telescopic baton dangling from her waist.

As we entered the room Angell's eyes wandered over us with detached curiosity but Nicki sat forward in her seat, shoulders stiffening. She was wearing shiny black leggings, a flimsy red top (in spite of the cold) and the highest heels I had ever seen. There were several large bruises on her upper arms and long scratches down her neck, one of them glistening with spots of red. Her cheeks were sunken and there was a slightly wild glint in her eyes as they travelled over me, scrutinising. A few bubbles of adrenaline announced their arrival in my stomach, which performed a small flip in greeting. 'Hello, Nicki,' I said, arranging my mouth into a smile. Staying close to the door as instructed, I leaned forwards into a half-crouch and softened my voice. 'And hello there, Angell. I'm Rosie.'

Angell stared at me blankly but Nicki took a sharp breath in response and continued the unabashed inspection. Her mouth twisted as her eyes ran over me, the silver ring through her bottom lip temporarily disappearing from view. 'I still don't understand why you can't sort somewhere for both of us,' Nicki barked, eyeing Jo resentfully. Her voice was deep and croaky, as if she'd just woken up.

Jo inhaled and then took a full ten seconds to blow the breath out. I wondered whether she was silently counting to herself, one of my trusty old tricks when patience was running thin. 'We've been through this, Nicki. You need to be seen by a doctor and the on-duty social worker wants to do an assessment before you're allowed to take Angell home.'

Nicki scowled and muttered something under her breath. She scraped at her teeth with an extraordinarily long fingernail, examined the haul and then snapped her eyes back to me. 'You got other kids?' she asked sharply, running a hand roughly across her forehead. It lingered there for a moment before trailing down her face and pulling on her jaw.

Mesmerised by the jazzy decorations stuck to her finger-nails, I hesitated for a moment then countered her stare with a steady gaze of my own. 'Yes, I have a daughter who's 16,' I said brightly, hoping to lighten the tension. 'And then there's Jamie, he's 12. They both love younger children so they'll be thrilled to meet Angell.'

Her demeanour altered slightly, the stubborn slant of her chin softening just a fraction. I put her somewhere in her early twenties, at most, though her wolfish scowl reminded me of a much younger, defensive teenager.

'Angell don't like nuffink hot for dinner,' she warned, 'nor the dark neither.'

'I'll bear that in mind,' I said softly.

A moment later Angell yawned and then gave a little moan, wriggling on his mother's lap in search of a snug position to sleep. With his roughly chopped but wavy dark hair and big eyes, he was a beautifully delicate-looking child. His Ben 10 tracksuit was rolled back several times at the cuffs and on his feet he wore a pair of black, frayed trainers that looked far too clumpy for him. Beyond tired, his head flopped wearily against his mother's chest and another small cry escaped his lips. The sight set off an itch in me: a strong desire to give him a hug and make him comfortable.

'Right,' Jo said briskly. 'We need to get this little chap sorted. He's exhausted. Is there anything else you'd like to ask the foster carer before she leaves?'

Nicki's eyes flicked towards the door as if considering her options but then she looked back at Jo and her shoulders sagged in defeat. The officer approached but Nicki jerked away and then flinched as if in pain. She took in a sharp breath and rubbed her side.

'Not yet,' she snapped, flattening her hand against the air. 'You lot make me sick, going round taking everyone's kid off 'em all the time. Baby snatchers, that's what you are.'

'We have to have good reason, Nicki,' Jo said with feigned patience. 'And we certainly don't take everyone's baby. It's rare for us to remove children actually.'

'No it ain't,' Nicki shouted, adamant. Her chin jutted out aggressively. 'Everyone I know has 'ad a kid taken off 'em.'

At first her comment struck me as grossly exaggerated, but then I realised that not everyone shares the same version of reality. It was quite possible that, in Nicki's world, there was a heavy involvement with social services and so, from her perspective, it might not have been such a stretch of the imagination.

Nicki whispered something into Angell's ear and he pulled back, eyes widening in horror. Pointing in my direction, she nodded and spoke louder, her tone reassuring but insistent. Angell glanced at me and began to cry, clinging tightly to Nicki's shoulders. She stroked his hair, a loving gesture from someone who seemed so volatile. After cupping his face in her hands and planting a gentle kiss on his nose, she gave Jo a bitter stare. For a moment, as the officer leaned forwards, I thought that Nicki looked dangerously close to lashing out.

My throat constricted and my ears pounded as I braced myself for an ugly struggle. It was a surprise, then, when Jo slipped her hands under Angell's arms, to see Nicki gently easing him away.

On separation, Angell's chest puffed out and he began to pant, his mouth falling open in terror. I waited for the resultant wail but, although his face contorted, no sound escaped him. With tears streaming down his cheeks, he pummelled the air with his fists. Clearly desperate to get back to his mother, it was strangely disconcerting to see that his protest remained silent. Distraught, Nicki spoke rapidly, her voice trembling but supplicating. It's rare for a foster carer to be present at the moment a child is removed. Most placements are carefully planned so we usually only witness the aftermath, but in emergency situations gentle introductions are rarely possible. Seeing Angell's mouth distorted in panic and his eyes full of fear had a profound impact on me. The violence of the act really hit me then, more than ever before.

Two More Sleeps

Looking back on our short time with Angell, it was his wordless protest that unsettled me most of all. Despite all the revelations that were to emerge in the coming days, my abiding memory is his silent, horrified reaction. Even now, when I picture it, the hair on the back of my neck tingles.

I reached out sideways as Jo thrust Angell towards me, trying to protect my stomach from his wild kicks. He struggled as I fastened him to my side, his arms flailing wildly. Spinning around, I caught a glimpse of Nicki. With her hand clamped over her mouth and tears running over her fingers, she suddenly looked vulnerable and lost. It seemed like any words I had to say would sound empty but I wanted to give her one last look of reassurance before I left. 'I'll keep him safe, I promise,' I said as Jo propelled me towards the door, hoping Nicki would take solace in that.

She rose to her feet. 'Hey, you? Wait, there's something you should know.'

'Sit down!' Jo commanded, waving her back. 'Go!' she barked at me.

The thick-set custody officer appeared in front of me. 'This way, love,' he said, cupping my elbow and leading me briskly towards the outer door.

'What's that face for?' he bellowed at Angell as he opened the first security door. Trying his best to jolly Angell out of his despair, the sergeant kept up a steady chatter all the way up the stairs and along the corridor. I knew he was trying to be kind but I found myself speeding up to try and get rid of him sooner. He didn't seem to notice that every time he spoke, Angell's hysteria ratcheted up a level.

Back in reception I thanked the officer and told him I could manage without him. He gave me a doubtful look, wished me a Merry Christmas and then, thankfully, left us alone. 'It's alright, sweetie,' I crooned to Angell, trying to sound as convincing as possible. Clasping him to my middle I slumped down on the wooden bench and wrestled with the duffel bag, trying to get his new coat out. Taking advantage of my compromised position, Angell wriggled away, managing to get his feet to the floor. The extra leverage helped and he slipped free, scrambling for the door. Dropping the bag, I dived after him and clamped a hand around his wrist.

'Nooooo!' he wailed, squirming away. His face was swollen and puce. My arms went weak with the effort of holding him and I worried that I was squeezing so hard I might leave a mark behind. 'I'm not going to hurt you, honey. You're safe, you're quite safe.'

Feeling like a kidnapper, I decided to give up on the coat and get him to the car as quickly as possible. Heaving the bag over my shoulder, I ignored his kicks and clamped him tightly to me, my arms trembling with the effort. When we reached the door, a marked car pulled around the corner and crossed our path, its blue lights reflecting silently on the icy tarmac.

The sight of the car and the shock of the cold had an arresting effect on Angell. With his breath fogging in front of him, he stopped struggling for a moment. I snatched the opportunity, repositioning him on my hip and then taking the stone steps carefully, one at a time. 'It's alright, honey,' I said breathlessly, knowing he was unlikely to trust a word I said.

Somewhere in the distant yard, an off-duty police dog barked mournfully. The haunting sound roused Angell and his writhing grew more frantic, his soundless screams escalating into breathless hysteria. My heart hammered as his protests continued, his fingernails digging into the skin of my neck. I picked up my pace so that I was almost running.

Less than a minute away from the car he began to lose momentum, his terror giving way to sorrowful tears. The wind suddenly picked up but I was grateful for it; Angell no longer fought but clung to me like a baby koala to its mother, his head nestling into the soft woollen loops of my scarf.

Despite his exhaustion, Angell remained awake throughout the journey home. As if the widening distance between himself and his mother had weakened his courage to protest, he sat passively in the back of the car, a steady stream of tears running down his cheeks. In the rear-view mirror I could see his frail shoulders trembling with each sob and my heart went out to him. Longing to pick him up and give him a hug, I drove a fraction over the speed limit, grateful that, being Christmas Eve, the roads were unusually empty. We arrived home just as afternoon was turning to evening.

Indoors, Angell gave another silent howl when I removed his trainers then rejected my attempts to comfort him, curling himself up on the floor between the sofa and a bookshelf. Every time I went anywhere near him he whimpered, cowering away from me with such fear that I felt like the child catcher. The sad thing was, when I left the room to get him a drink, he shuffled after me, knowing he had no choice but to attach himself to the nearest adult. It wasn't really surprising that he was fearful of me; within minutes of meeting him I had pinned him to my side and refused to return him to his mother – not the most gentle of introductions.

My mum, knowing it would be best to filter the outside world for a short while, slipped home without introducing herself. My whole family were due to come to me for Christmas dinner, so Angell would meet her the next day. I knew how overwhelmed he was likely to be with all the commotion and if it were any other occasion I would have rescheduled, but how could I cancel Christmas?

Emily and Jamie waved their grandma off at the door and then walked quietly into the living room, Emily crouching and whispering a soft hello. Angell stared at them with wide eyes full of misery. 'Aw, it's alright,' Emily said tenderly. 'You're safe here.'

Angell retreated, burying his head into a cushion. His shoulders began trembling with fresh sobs. I knew Emily was probably itching to give him a hug but when she glanced at me I said quietly: 'Maybe we should give Angell a bit of space.' She nodded knowingly and sat next to her brother at the other end of the sofa. They tried to behave naturally but their eyes kept flicking over to him, their expressions filled with concern. 'He knows we're here if he needs us,' I added, more for Angell's ears than theirs. And then, hoping to distract everyone and lighten the tension, I asked if they'd managed to wrap the presents I had bought for him earlier that day.

'Yep,' Jamie answered, 'all done. And we've been to the shops to get some mince pies for Father Christmas.' He glanced towards Angell again and I realised he was making a renewed effort to get him involved, bless him.

At 16 and 12, Emily and Jamie were well past believing that Christmas presents arrived on a sleigh but with little ones in residence they would regress, throwing themselves into all the festive delights.

'Have we got any carrots for Rudolph?' Emily asked theatrically. 'Reindeers love them.'

'Hmmm, yes, I think so.'

Angell raised his head a fraction at that, watching us surreptitiously from beneath his dark fringe. Our talk seemed to bring him back to himself, his locked, numb expression fading. Jamie spotted his interest and turned to speak to him but I shook my head minutely. Children are often hardened against the world when they first arrive in the foster home, their small bodies rigid with stress. I've found that it usually works best to leave them alone for a short time. Once they've acclimatised they tend to reach out of their own accord.

Sure enough, within half an hour, Angell was sitting on the floor beside the Christmas tree, watching as Emily and

Jamie sorted the presents into piles. With a rising, 'And-d-d-d-d,' Jamie shifted a large pile of unevenly wrapped parcels across the floor to Angell. 'Guess who these are for?' Angell stared up at him with watery brown eyes, his only response a heavy, hiccoughy sigh.

Emily crouched in front of him. 'Shall we shake the presents and see if we can guess what's in them?' she asked enticingly.

Angell cocked his head to one side, considering, but then gave a tiny shake of his head.

Not one to be beaten, Jamie disappeared from the room and came back a few minutes later with his old garage and a box of cars.

Emily immediately pounced, her hands finding her hips. 'And why did you have to bring those down, Jamie?' she demanded. 'Just because he's a boy doesn't mean he'll like cars, you know.'

'Oh no, she's off again, Mum,' Jamie groaned. Ever since Emily had started analysing feminist texts at school we were subjected to regular lectures about the inherent sexism in society. She would rage about it, and, while I appreciated her passion, it sometimes wore a bit thin.

'I'm just saying, Jamie, that if you reinforce gender roles when children are little you're casting the die and there's no going back.'

Jamie started humming loudly, his fingers in his ears. I tensed, hoping Angell wouldn't pick up on the conflict. Fortunately he glanced between them impassively, probably too lost in his own trauma to be affected by anything else.

'If people would stop stereotyping children, maybe boys would grow up to be a bit more responsible and stop causing carnage around the world.'

Making a point of ignoring his sister's increasingly screechy tone, Jamie lifted a Matchbox car high above his head. 'Look what I've got, Angell.'

'Jamie, you're so –'

'Emily …' I said, warningly, with a tilt of my head towards Angell. She opened her mouth to go on another rant but thankfully thought better of it.

Jamie swooped the car through the air. 'Wow, look, Angell. See how cool this is? Vrrmm …'

It was a spirited attempt but the little boy wasn't impressed. He lowered his chin and stared mournfully at the floor.

'See, I told you.' Emily stalked out to the cupboard under the stairs and returned with a box of dolls and some little clothes. She knelt beside Angell and pulled a few dolls out, one with a leg missing. 'Look, we can play hospitals with these, Angell. Shall we make the dolly better?'

Amazingly, Angell's eyebrows tilted upwards and his lips opened a fraction – nowhere near a smile, but he was definitely interested. Emily, triumphant, couldn't resist crowing. 'Ha! See, Jamie.'

Jamie made a clicking noise at the back of his throat as if Angell had let the team down. He slumped down on the sofa and switched the television on in disgust.

I felt a flare of gratitude towards Emily – it was such a relief to see Angell livening up. Peering into the toy box, his fingers twitched with temptation. When he finally summoned the courage to delve in, I noticed how well he handled the toys. Children often come into care with no idea how to play and, until they learn, they can be a bit destructive. Clearly, someone had spent time playing with Angell.

As I watched him, the mystery of his abandonment deepened. I combed over the last few hours, trying to grasp some clues as to what could have led a seemingly loving mother to behave so irresponsibly. I got the strangest sensation that I was missing something, but I couldn't pinpoint what it was. Seeing Angell so distressed yet unable to make a sound had been disconcerting, and then there were Nicki's parting words. What was it she had said? 'There's something you should know.' My mind kept snagging on them, certain that she had been readying herself to warn me about something.

As Angell tucked the one-legged doll into a box and covered her gently with a small blanket, I pictured Nicki's face as she released her little boy. Clearly bereft, she had relinquished him peacefully to spare him the trauma of being fought over; a loving, selfless act. It was another little detail to add to a puzzle where none of the pieces seemed to fit.

Having relaxed a little, by 6 p.m. Angell was able to drink some juice but at the mention of dinner he grew tearful again. Remembering what Nicki had said about hot food, I led him by the hand and let him rifle through the fun-size boxes of cereal in one of my cupboards. Sitting on the floor, he tore at the cardboard top of a pack of corn-flakes and stuck his hand in, cramming the flakes into his mouth.

I reached for the box. 'I think we'll pour them into a bowl now, shall we Angell?'

His lip wobbled, silent tears spilling onto his cheeks.

'It's alright, sweetie. Look, you can help me if you like.' I set a bowl on the floor between his legs and returned the cereal box to him. 'There we are, you tip them in. And then we'll get some milk.'

Angell stared up at me and shook his head, his eyes swollen with fat tears. Knowing when to pick my battles, I made a placating noise and let him stick his hand back inside. Within a minute the box was empty. He reached for another one, ripping at the lid and tearing at the cellophane inside with his teeth. As long as he drank a glass of milk, I reasoned, there wasn't too much wrong with the basic meal.

After their little play, Angell seemed much more comfortable with Emily than with me. When I held my hand out and suggested that it was time for a bath, Angell thrust himself at Emily and wrapped his arms tightly around her neck. She beamed. 'I could come as well, if that helps?' she suggested.

'Yes, good idea.'

Upstairs in the bathroom, Angell sat on the floor next to Emily and wrapped his arms around himself, lips quivering at the suggestion of getting undressed. 'You need to have a bath, Angell,' Emily said. 'You smell like wet dog.'

He chuckled at that, a real belly laugh. When he caught me looking at him and smiling, his mouth clamped shut.

Taking advantage of the moment I knelt behind him and gently tugged him to his feet. Emily pulled funny faces at him and as I lifted his tracksuit top over his head she said, 'Boo!' He giggled again and, grateful for the distraction, I slipped his bottoms and pants down to his ankles.

On automatic pilot, my eyes travelled over his back to check for any marks or bruises, something foster carers are advised to do whenever a new child arrives. I was so absorbed in the examination that I barely noticed Emily's gasp.

It only registered when she said: 'Er, Mum?'

Rising to a crouch, I peered over Angell's left shoulder and saw that Emily was staring at Angell's midriff, her lips twisted in bewilderment.

I felt a spasm of anxiety, hoping she hadn't spotted a cigarette burn or something even nastier. 'What is it?'

Angell eyes darted between us, wide in alarm.

'Well, look for yourself,' Emily said, putting her hands on his shoulders and gently turning him around to face me. 'I think you'll find there's something missing.'

I ran my eyes over Angell's torso then clamped a hand to my forehead in surprise. I couldn't quite believe what I was seeing. Emily was correct – there certainly was something missing, if Angell was really a boy. 'Well, well, well,' I said in a sing-song voice, trying to project an air of calm. Having picked up on our shock, Angell's bottom lip was wobbling with fear. 'It's alright, Angell, there's nothing to worry about. We adults seem to have got our wires crossed, that's all. Let's get you into the bath now, sweetheart.'

It took a while to coax Angell into bed. She kept asking me to take her back to her mum, clasping her hands together at one point and pleading. My heart lurched. However much I explained that I was taking care of her for a short time while Mummy saw a doctor, she just couldn't seem to take it in. It was almost 8 p.m. when she finally surrendered and sank down onto my lap.

I stroked her back and read her a story, thinking what a shame it was that she had nothing from home to comfort her. At least with planned placements, children have one or two familiar bits to cling on to but Angell had nothing, not even her own pyjamas. To make matters worse, everything I had bought for her earlier in the day was covered in dinosaurs or Power Rangers. Ignoring Emily's protests, I had whipped the Fireman Sam duvet cover from the bed and replaced it with a Disney princess one but Angell was no happier with the change. She seemed so immensely sad, her tears starting again as soon as we reached the end of the book. 'Right, let's tuck you in,' I said, holding out my hand to help her up. She flinched, backing away – I was the last person she wanted help from. Standing on tiptoes, she threw the top half of her body onto the mattress and, clasping a handful of duvet, heaved herself up.

I sat on the floor while she wriggled herself under the duvet, wondering again why her mother had disguised her. It seemed such a strange thing to do but I suspected that, whatever the reason, the motivation would have been one of love. Every now and then Angell glanced at me, her forehead furrowed, as if trying to work out what I was up to. Clearly she still didn't trust me, but every time I made a move to leave she whimpered. Her limbs and neck were stiff with tension, and soothing the pain of being wrenched from her mother was out of my reach, no matter how many hugs I offered.

I stayed beside her until the tension ebbed away, her head falling limp against the pillow.

Downstairs, I could hear Jamie's crowing from the hallway. 'Why can't you just admit you were wrong? Angell likes dolls because she's a girl. If she had been a boy she would have wanted to play with the cars.'

I hovered in the doorway of the living room, watching as Emily's face crumpled in on itself. Her hands migrated to her hips, a sure sign of her fury. 'Well, you loved wearing dresses when you were a toddler. Your favourite was a sparkly pink one and you used to cry when Mum put it in the wash. You wore it to Pizza Hut once.'

'Yeah, right. Course I did.'

Sheepishly, I sidestepped Emily, trying to make it to the kitchen unseen. She swung around. 'He did wear that dress out, didn't he? Do you remember?'

'Um ...'

'I did not! She's lying, Mum, isn't she?'

I paused.

Jamie stared at me in horror. 'You let me go out in a dress?!'

'Well, you wore a coat on top,' I said weakly. 'You didn't want to take it off.'

He clapped a hand to his forehead and groaned.

'Ha!' Emily gloated in delight. 'And I've got a photo somewhere. I'm going to find it and show everyone tomorrow.'

'You can't let her do that, Mum!'

'Emily, stop it. It's Christmas Eve.'

She continued to snicker so I distracted her by inviting her to help me sort through the storage boxes under the stairs. I wanted to find a few toys that Angell hadn't seen that would appeal to a girl of her age. There were some gender-neutral presents wrapped up under the tree but most of the toys I had bought the previous day were aimed at boys. While searching, Emily gave me one of her lectures for worrying about it, 'You'll be doing Angell a favour by giving her boy toys. Didn't you know that girls who are given traditionally male toys score higher in intelligence tests?'

'Well, how about that?' I said mildly, reaching for a small buggy folded up at the back of the cupboard. I didn't necessarily disagree with Emily but Angell had clearly enjoyed playing with the dolls – I just wished we had something new that I knew she would like.

We managed to rescue a few old bits – the buggy still worked fine and there was a small bear with a satchel full of teddy clothes, but if I'm honest they were all a bit raggedy.

As we wrapped the moribund finds Emily said: 'Oh, by the way, a police officer called while you were upstairs. She wanted to let you know that Angell's mum is starting to open up and he is really a she. I told her we made that discovery ourselves.'

I grinned. 'We certainly did.'

Emily secured a label on one of the gifts with a piece of sticky tape and then sat back on her haunches, frowning. 'Why do you think she made out that Angell was a boy?'

'I don't know,' I said slowly, although several motives were beginning to bubble through my mind. I knew it was quite possible that I was way off kilter – the only certainty when fostering is that each day holds a promise of the unexpected.

I slept well that night, but my dreams were a jumble of confusion, skipping randomly through the events of the day. The draconian brutality of Angell's separation from her mother kept playing on a loop in my unconscious mind, coupled with the strengthening conviction that Nicki wasn't all that she seemed.

Jenny, one of my fostering friends, kept floating in and out of my thoughts as well. As is our usual tradition, we exchanged texts late in the evening, wishing each other a peaceful day ahead. Christmas is rarely an easy celebration for children in care – the day being a painful reminder of their own absent family – and I knew that Jenny was anticipating a particularly difficult time. Twelve-year-old Justin had moved in with the foster carer just two weeks earlier and she was still struggling to contain his violent behaviour.

Over the last couple of years, Jenny, I and two other local carers had met up regularly and, having witnessed each other sobbing at one point or another, the usual barriers to intimacy seemed to have crumbled away. I felt completely at ease in their company and knew that word of my new placement would travel quickly around our small group.

What I hadn't expected, though, was their response. I had set my alarm for 5 a.m., eager to put Jamie Oliver's advice of preparing the dinner hours before cooking into practice. With everything ready to pop into the oven, I would be able to spend lots of time nursing Angell through what was likely to be a stressful day for her – that was the theory, anyway.

It was still dark when I crept downstairs but even without the lights on I noticed a white note suspended halfway through the letter box. Intrigued, I released it gently and quickly unfolded it.

Rosie,
Heard about the mix-up – I recently bought some new bits for After School Club but we don't start over again until 6 Jan so plenty of time to replace them. Hope this helps.
  Enjoy your day!
  Rachel x

With a little skip in my chest I reached for my keys and, trying not to rattle them, stepped over the plate of mince pies and carrots on the mat and unlocked the door. There, piled high in a wicker basket on the path just below the front step, were several gifts gorgeously wrapped in pink and purple sparkly paper. I clapped my hands to my cheeks, overwhelmed by Rachel's thoughtfulness.

Excitedly, I carried the frost-covered basket into the living room. As I unpacked the presents I noticed that Rachel had attached a photo of the contents to the outside of the wrapping with a slither of tape. It was unbelievably thoughtful of her and I was still buzzing with gratitude as I peeled the potatoes and prepared the stuffing balls. It had been such a wonderful start to the day that my worries about how Angell would cope were pushed firmly to the back of my mind. Getting into the Christmas spirit, I opened a caramel and cinnamon syrup, added a dash to some coffee and sat down on the bottom stair to listen out for her.

Gone were the days when Jamie would leap out of bed at 5 a.m. pleading to open his presents. Excitement usually still got the better of Emily, who tended to hibernate the other 364 days of the year, but at 6.30 a.m. both of them were still holed up in their rooms. There was still no sound from Angell either so at 7 a.m., after nibbling a few reindeer bites in the carrots and crumbling one of the mince pies, I crept up the stairs to check on her. I stopped short in the doorway of her room, surprised to find her softly weeping, her thumb in her mouth.

Her head snapped up when she saw me. She frowned, as if she couldn't quite place who I was. I felt a pang of guilt

– while I'd been enjoying my coffee she'd been alone and crying in a strange house. 'Morning,' I said softly, kneeling beside her and reaching out to stroke the sleep-knotted tendrils of dark hair that were clinging to her wet cheeks. 'How long have you been awake?'

She sat up and rubbed her damp eyes. They were red-rimmed and swollen; she must have been crying for quite some time. 'I don't want dis room,' she quavered, her bottom lip trembling. 'I want Mummy's room.'

'I know, sweetie, I know.' I wished I could tell her how many sleeps it would be until her first contact session with Nicki, but I had no idea and, being Christmas, I didn't expect to hear anything from social services for at least a couple of days. 'Someone will arrange for you to see Mummy soon, I promise. Now, shall we go downstairs and see if the reindeers ate their carrots?'

The crease in her brow deepened and she gave a little sorrowful shake of her head. Temporarily stumped, I was trying to figure out how to persuade her to join me when Emily burst into the room. 'Morning! It's Christmas, hooray!' She knelt beside me and kissed my cheek. Angell held her breath mid-sob, staring up at Emily in surprise.

'Happy Christmas, Mum! You too, Angell. Come on, let's go and open the presents.' Emily grabbed Angell's hand, pulled her to her feet and swept her from the room. 'Come on, Mum,' she said impatiently, banging on Jamie's door on the way to the stairs. 'Jamie! Get up, it's Christmas!'

It was at times like this that I realised, even after years of fostering, that there was still so much I needed to learn about children. I sat for a moment and stared after them, smiling and shaking my head.

Our guests began arriving around midday. Thanks to Jamie Oliver, dinner was coming along nicely, so much so that when my mum arrived I was able to decline all offers of help and spend some time introducing her to Angell. Within minutes, Angell was curled up next to Mum on the sofa, still wearing the Ben 10 tracksuit she had arrived in. I had tried to coax her into wearing some of her new clothes but, understandably, she wanted to keep the few things that were familiar close by. Thankfully I had thrown everything into the washing machine when she went to bed, so at least it was clean. One by one, Angell showed my mum the toys she had opened earlier that morning. Every one of Rachel's gifts had been a hit and Angell had spent the morning dragging them along on a blanket behind her as she followed me from room to room.

It was a relief to see her reaching out to Mum for comfort, but part of me felt a failure for not being the one providing it. As they flicked through the pages of a *Little Mermaid* book, Angell smiling and leaning into Mum's arm, I told myself that her rejection wasn't personal – in her eyes I was a usurper, the one responsible for snatching her away from her mum. It would take time for her to realise that I was firmly on her side.

With her safe haven marked out on the sofa next to Mum, Angell barely raised an eyebrow as the rest of the guests turned up – my aunt and uncle, youngest brother

and his family and Mary, an elderly ex-neighbour of mine
– although when Chris, my effusive older brother, arrived
with his wife and three sons, she clasped her toys a little
closer, chin quivering. Bounding into the living room,
Chris pulled me into a bone-crushing hug, exchanged a
noisy high-five with Jamie then chased Emily around with
his arms thrown wide. 'Come and give your Uncle Chris a
big cuddle.'

'Urgh, get off!' Emily giggled, waving him away. Emily
and Jamie appreciate their uncle's unreserved enthusiasm
and cheerful banter these days, but when they were small,
his loud, gravelly voice left them wide-eyed and slightly
tearful.

Chris laughed and gave up, his eyes finally landing on
Angell.

He leaned over and slapped his hands on his thighs. 'Oh,
hello, little one. I didn't notice you there.' Bestowing a
tickle to her tummy he said: 'You must be Angell.'

Angell looked up tremulously and leaned closer to my
mum.

I cupped a hand in a C-shape around my mouth. 'Um,
boundaries, Chris,' I hissed, 'boundaries ...' When I began
fostering I explained to my family that foster carers have a
responsibility to ensure that the children in their care will not
be tickled. Having expressed their unanimous opinion ('what
piffle!') they agreed to rein in their tactile natures, promptly
forgetting whenever said children were in placement.

'Oh, stop worrying, Rosie. She's alright, aren't you,
Angell? Looks like you've got some lovely presents there.'

Angell looked into his open face with a look of puzzlement and then, amazingly, the edges of her mouth curled upwards. Thinking she was on the verge of a smile, I felt a surge of happiness, but then, after a sidelong glance at me, she leaned forwards and whispered into Chris's ear, 'Will *you* take me back to Mummy?'

My heart sank with the realisation that she had been wearing a look of hope. Chris glanced at me then crouched in front of her. 'Aw, you're staying with Rosie for a while, darling,' he said, his bristly face soft with compassion. 'She'll take good care of you.'

Her eyes filled up and she turned away, burying her face into my mum's shoulder.

By 2 p.m., with the dinner almost ready and the house filled with happy conversation, I was enticed into a false sense of security. Every so often Angell would tug at the sleeve of a passing relative and ask them when she could see her mum, hoping to get a different answer from the one I kept giving – 'soon, sweetie, soon' – but apart from that, she seemed to be coping brilliantly, unperturbed by all the unfamiliar faces and sudden bursts of laughter. My plan was for us all to eat together at the table and then, at 3 p.m., watch the Queen's Speech with Christmas pudding in bowls on our laps.

Unfortunately, Angell had other ideas.

As soon as Mum took her hand and led her to the table, her shoulders begin to shake, tears rolling down her cheeks. My heart melted but I was so busy trying to get everyone squeezed around our small table (niftily extended with an 8-ft block of MDF planted on top of it, disguised with shiny Christmas paper) that I left my mum to coax her along. The trouble was that, within seconds, several well-meaning adults had circled, all trying to offer their own form of comfort.

Angell shook her head in panic, utterly bewildered. 'How about we sit over here?' Mum said, shooing everyone away and settling herself on the chair in the corner. Angell leaned into her, making no sound but weeping as if she was grief-stricken. It was such a strange sight – her mouth wide open in a silent howl, eyes full of sorrow.

I suspected that she was used to restraining herself, perhaps fearful of making a noise at home. Her reticence reminded me of Catie, a one-year-old who came to stay with us a few years earlier. Alarm bells rang when Catie's social worker described her as a docile baby who 'wasn't any trouble'. While it was true that Catie never cried, it wasn't because she was a 'good' baby. I think she had simply learnt the cruel lesson that however much she cried, no one would come to lift her out of her cot.

'Dig in everyone, don't wait for me,' Mum said brightly. 'We'll be alright in a minute, won't we, Angell?'

Angell buried her head into Mum's shoulder. I was hoping that, if we all ignored her, she might feel less conspicuous and begin to relax. A couple of minutes later though, she had wriggled from my mum's lap and was crouching at her feet beneath the table. It was difficult to know what to do. I wanted to include her but, knowing it was perhaps a bit too much to expect, I decided to let her stay where she was. No child can eat under duress and, from what her mum had said, she wasn't used to eating hot food anyway. While I wasn't going to give her a packet of crisps for Christmas lunch, I planned to offer her a sandwich or some fruit when she had calmed down.

The funny thing was that as it turned out, there was no need for snacks. After a few minutes I noticed a pair of eyes peering over the table ledge opposite. I ignored them and carried on talking to my sister-in-law, hoping Angell's peek would develop into a full-blown appearance. A moment later though, a hand emerged, walking itself across the table towards one of the bowls of leftovers. Within seconds, the small fingers had curled around a roast potato and then quickly withdrawn, like one of those grabbing plastic hands from a children's money box. I decided not to draw attention to it. At least she was eating and, with all the commotion in the house, it was hardly the right time to start setting boundaries.

Much to the stifled amusement of my family, the hand worked its way through a wide selection of foods from the side dishes, both hot and cold. I might have found the sight comical as well, if it hadn't been quite so sad.

It was lovely, having the whole family together around our table, but throughout the meal I couldn't stop my thoughts drifting away from them. I kept wondering whether Nicki was still in hospital and, if not, how she would spend the day away from her daughter. Was it the first Christmas they had been apart, I wondered. I knew Angell was probably still too wary of me to open up about her home life, even if she had been able to find the words. Fortunately, the past seems to have a canny knack of revealing itself.

Around 4 p.m., with a wink in my mum's direction, I went upstairs. My aunt, who was to be 70 on Boxing Day, had recently discovered a passion for art and so we had clubbed together to buy her an easel with all the associated paraphernalia. I had hidden it away in my bedroom but it was so heavy that I needed a hand to carry it down.

Angell, still firmly attached to my mum's side, came along as well. Chris followed her in and I handed the largest package, the easel, to him, and a couple of the smaller boxes to my mum. I turned, intending to pass Angell one of the smaller gifts, a set of brushes, so that she'd feel included, but she had disappeared.

My mum spun around on her heel. 'She was here a second ago!'

Even though I knew she couldn't have gone far, I felt uneasiness creeping over me. 'Angell, where are you?'

After lifting the duvet and checking behind the curtains, we turned a few futile circles and then, just as we were about to leave the room, we heard a tiny sniff. It seemed to be coming from the wardrobe. Chris, Mum and I exchanged baffled looks and I pulled the door open. There, huddled in the back of the wardrobe with one of my jumpers clutched to her face, was Angell. 'I didn't look,' she said tearfully, her voice muffled by the wool. 'Has he done yet? Is he gone?'

I looked back at Mum with raised eyebrows. She winked and squeezed my arm. 'We'll leave you to it,' she whispered, following Chris out of the room. I knelt on the floor and swept the clothes that were hanging over Angell to one side. The rail above her head screeched in protest and Angell flinched, silent screams erupting from her throat again.

'It's alright, there's nothing to be scared of, love,' I said softly, but she was so fearful that it took several minutes to coax her out. I took her hand, helping her to her feet, and noticed how clammy it was. Absolutely terrified, her face was scarlet. She took deep, gulping breaths.

'I can see that you're frightened, Angell,' I said, putting words to her feelings in the hope that she would recognise that I was in tune with her. 'Can you tell me why?' I ventured.

She gulped, her chest heaving as she tried to calm herself. I sat back on my feet and drew her onto my lap. Surprisingly, she submitted, pressing her warm back against my chest. She looked up at me with big eyes. 'Is nuver man coming yet?'

I frowned. 'Sorry, honey?'

'Shall I hide again before nuver one comes?'

'No one else is coming up here, Angell,' I said slowly, the truth behind Nicki's abandonment of her daughter beginning to take shape in my mind. 'Chris came in to help collect the presents, that's all.'

Angell's eyes flitted between the door and the wardrobe, unsure whether to trust my word. I rubbed her back and swayed, the events of Christmas Eve coalescing into a feasible scenario. I knew that, if I was anywhere near the truth, Nicki was going to need all the help she could get if she was to stand a chance of getting her little girl back.

'Do you know what I do when I'm feeling unhappy or scared, Angell?' I asked, wrapping my arms around her middle and rocking slightly. Her head was tucked beneath my chin, her hair tickling my skin as she shook her head. 'I imagine that I have a special balloon that I can climb into whenever I want. It can float through the air or rest on the ground but do you know what's really special about it?'

She shook her head again, glancing sideways at me.

'Well, it's made of glass, so not only can I hear what everyone around me is saying but I can see everything as well. I tuck myself away, warm and safe, and I stay in there for as long as I want to.'

Her breathing began to slow as she stared at me, one eyebrow cocked.

I smiled and her lips twitched, almost responding with one of her own. 'And do you know what's even more special?'

'What?' she asked in a croaky, mucus-filled voice.

'Anyone can have a balloon like that.'

She frowned, thinking about it for a minute. 'Can I have one?'

'Yes. It's ready for you, whenever you need it.'

'I can get in it now, can I?'

I nodded. 'Yes, if you want to.'

We walked downstairs together, Angell moving roboti-cally, as if she was frightened her balloon might be too fragile to take her weight. She spent the next hour or so in a trance-like state, quietly removed from the merriment going on around her.

It wasn't until after 7 p.m. that I noticed the home tele-phone flashing with a recorded message. Pressing my right hand flat against my ear to drown out the sound of *Strictly Come Dancing* in the background, I pressed play and leaned my head against the wall, listening. It was a duty social worker with a strong Liverpudlian accent, who introduced himself as Ben. 'Hello, Rosie, sorry to disturb you on Christmas Day but I need to talk to you about Angell.'

I straightened, a wave of anticipation rushing over me.

'We've had some, um,' there was a pause, and then the light male voice issued through the air again, 'enlightening disclosures from Mum.'

I held myself still, readying myself.

'I won't go into detail here. Can you call me as soon as you can, please?' He left a mobile number and then cut off, the message ending with a resounding buzz. An automated voice announced the time of the call – 1.05 p.m. I pressed my lips together and played the message again, scribbling the mobile number he'd left on the back of my hand and then quickly dialling it. There was a click and then Ben's voice regurgitated a standard 'Sorry I'm not available right now' message. Frustrated, I sank back against the wall, immediately jumping away as the phone jangled into life.

'Rosie?'

'Yes, it's me. Ben?' I apologised for not picking up the message sooner.

'That's OK,' he said, his accent less pronounced than it had been in his message. 'I just wanted to give you the heads up, love, to keep you in the picture, like. Mum's still in Queen Mary's Hospital but I've been to see her this morning and what she told me put a very different light on things, I have to say.'

'Oh, right?'

'Yes. The thing is, Nicki was w-o-rking yesterday morning when Angell was found,' Ben said, 'if you get what I mean?'

'Ah-ha,' I said, 'yes, I see.' Ben's emphasis made it clear. The possibility had popped into my head when Angell had hidden herself in the wardrobe after seeing Chris in my bedroom. When she went on to ask about other men I had gathered I was on the right track. 'So she was nearby then?'

'No, that had been her plan – she takes Angell with her when she works, I'll tell you why in a minute – but the punter didn't stick to the rules. He dragged her off and she fought to keep Angell within sight, hence the pummelling she took. I expect you noticed.'

A sinking feeling in the pit of my stomach told me that Nicki's chances of getting Angell back were looking decidedly grim. Des, my supervising social worker, had told me soon after we first met that there were lots of mothers who earned a living from prostitution. Apparently, as long as the children were well cared for in all other respects and kept away from 'tricks', social services didn't intervene. Nicki had opened up and been honest, which in a way was a good thing, but the trouble was that, by admitting that she took Angell to 'work' with her, the authorities had proof that she wasn't safeguarding her daughter. I pictured Angell as she clung desperately to her mother on Christmas Eve and my heart lurched. 'Oh dear, poor Angell.'

'Hmmm, don't worry, Rosie. You haven't heard the half of it yet. It's not all bad news.'

'O-kay …' I said, noticing for the first time that it wasn't just Ben's accent that made him sound cheerful. There was a fighting spirit in his tone.

'I wasn't too hopeful either, when I first heard the facts. But then I heard what Nicki's been going through. Rosie, she's being run by her partner, Angell's dad. Nasty thug, by the sounds of it. He forced her to work right through her pregnancy and throughout the years since.'

'Oh no,' I cupped my hand to my brow, leaned my shoulder against the wall.

'He's highly manipulative and she's so terrified of him that she won't let Angell out of her sight. That's why she takes the child with her while she works – a screwed up way of being protective, but I can see where she's coming from, if you understand what I mean?'

'Well, yes, absolutely. That does put another slant on things. But why didn't she ask anyone for help?'

'She was convinced that Angell would be taken away from her.'

I sighed at the irony.

'Yes, it's taken a lot to convince her to trust us. You know, stalking has come a long way in the digital age, Rosie. It's not a case of calling someone and then hanging up any more. Her partner has used geo-location software, to pinpoint her exact whereabouts, and listening devices, planted into Angell's clothes. Whenever Nicki has made a run for it in the past, he's always managed to track her down.'

As Ben spoke, the fragmented thoughts that had been floating around in my head finally organised themselves into a mosaic I recognised, the last pieces of the jigsaw falling into place. I was pretty sure the reason Angell had been made to look like a boy was another misguided attempt to protect her from the attention of Nicki's clients. And Angell's silent protests suddenly made sense as well – heaven knows what she may have witnessed during her short life, but whenever she was distressed, it was probably unsafe to make a sound.

Before he ended the call Ben filled me in on the plans he had made during the day – he had found a room for Nicki in a women's refuge over two hundred miles away. She had agreed never to return home and had handed her mobile telephone over to police officers so that all tracking devices could be disabled. After leaving hospital she would be moved to a safe house and would wait there until Tuesday, the day after Boxing Day. Angell would join her there and together they would make the long journey towards their new life.

* * *

Spontaneous dancing and an appalling but loud Bruce Forsyth impression (courtesy of Chris) had broken out in the living room, so I asked Angell to join me in the kitchen where I could tell her the news. Sliding from the sofa, she carefully stretched her blanket over the carpet, arranged her toys one by one on top and then lifted one corner, dragging it behind her as she followed me.

'I've just been speaking to someone who is taking care of Mummy,' I said, crouching on the floor in front of her and holding one of her hands.

The blanket fell to the floor as her hand flew into her mouth. She frowned, nibbling at the skin of her knuckles with her teeth.

'It's alright, it's very good news. They told me that Mummy is feeling much better now and guess what?'

Her eyebrows lifted as she squeaked a breathless: 'What?'

'You're going back to stay with her very soon.'

She took a rapid breath in, clasped her hands together and performed a little jump. 'Yes! Ray! Ray!' she said, clapping and bobbing up and down on her toes. 'See Mummy, yay!'

I laughed. 'I can see you're happy about that! I'm happy too.'

And then she melted my heart, throwing her arms around my neck and holding tight. I drew her to me and straightened, lifting her up high and spinning around on my heel. When I set her back on her feet she looked up at me, her face finally free from fraught anxiety. 'So how long time is it till I can see Mummy, Rosie?'

Two More Sleeps

I held up my middle and forefinger. 'Two more sleeps, sweetie, that's all. And then it will be time to see Mummy.'

Observing a long-held Lewis family tradition, towards the end of the evening I invited everyone to join me in the garden to watch the launch of some Chinese lanterns. Angell, no longer my reluctant shadow, stood happily beside me on the patio, one of her gloved hands tucked into the warmth of my coat pocket. The air was crisp, a bitter wind extinguishing my brothers' initial attempts to get the lanterns airborne. Impatient, my nieces and nephews began a rhythmic clap. Angell looked up at me with uncertainty. With a nod of reassurance she joined in, stamping her feet into the bargain.

Soon ten fiery bulbs were suspended in the darkness above our garden. Enchanted by the flames, Angell's face was luminescent, her breath fogging as she gasped and cooed. The lanterns drifted quickly but it was so lovely to see her looking carefree that I could barely tear my eyes away from her. We stayed outside until the golden thread of lights faded, leaving just a faint, smoky footprint over the trees.

The journey to the safe house took over an hour, and every mile or two Angell, her new toys piled high on her lap, bobbed up and down in her booster seat and asked, 'Nearly Mummy time, Rosie?'

It was a relief to reach our destination: a large semi-detached house in an affluent suburban street with shiny bay windows and a herringbone drive. As I pulled up outside I noticed a slight twitch of one of the curtains upstairs and before I'd even cut the engine and retrieved my keys, the front door was opened. Nicki tore across the driveway towards us so I quickly climbed out, opened the rear door, swept Angell's toys from her lap and released her seat belt. 'Mummy!' Angell shrieked, clamouring out. Nicki swept her up in one swift movement and the pair clung to each other, Angell burying her head into her mother's neck.

'I love you so much, baby,' Nicki said with a little sob. I rubbed a circle on each of their backs and then walked back to the car to retrieve Angell's things. Inside the house, Angell remained glued to her mother's lap while Nicki showed me photos she had been given of the refuge they would soon be moving to. The hard lines of her face were softened with affection and her cheeks were crimson, eyes glistening. She was dressed in the same clothes that she had worn in the police station, but with her feet bare and a sweatshirt over the flimsy top, she looked much less fierce. Younger too, with her face free of make-up and her dark hair tied in two plaits, one resting on each shoulder. She seemed positive about the future and, with Angell clearly thrilled to be back in her arms, after about half an hour or so I made a move to leave.

Angell looked up sharply. 'I not coming with you,' she said, gripping Nicki's shoulders. 'I stay here!'

Nicki looked embarrassed but I laughed. 'Of course you are, sweetie. But thank you for spending some time at Rosie's house. We loved having you.'

'Angell,' Nicki said chidingly. 'Say goodbye nicely.'

Angell cocked her head, smiling shyly. She raised her hand in a little wave and then buried her face back into her mum's neck.

'Goodbye, Nicki. All the best, honey,' I said, patting her arm. I kissed the top of Angell's head and then headed for the door.

'Oh, just a minute, Rosie.' I turned to see Nicki peeling herself away from Angell. She grabbed a tiny white hand-bag and rummaged around, pulling out a bunch of keys. A moment later she was on her feet and crossing the room, Angell clinging to her leg as she went. She reached for my hand and pressed a small, sparkly object into my palm, cupping her other hand around mine and giving it a squeeze. 'Thank you for looking after Angell,' she said, her eyes misting over. I smiled, reaching out and squeezing her arm.

It was only when I reached my car that I took a proper look at what Nicki had given me. As I had guessed, it was a key-ring, the scratched plastic case housing a faded picture of Nicki with a new-born Angell cradled in her arms. I still treasure the impromptu gift, even though it's a little battered. When I think of all that Nicki had to leave behind to keep herself and her daughter safe, it can't have been easy to part with one of the few possessions she had managed to hold on to.

Angell's placement was one of the shortest I've ever had, but reuniting her with her mother and witnessing their joyous reaction is one of the fostering moments that I hold dear. It's such a privilege to be able to offer a soft landing to a child during a low point in their life, a moment of tranquillity away from the stress they've known. When that moment's rest becomes a bridge towards a better life, being part of the transition is all the more rewarding.

ROSIE LEWIS

Unexpected

A True
Short Story

Unexpected

All things considered, it couldn't really get any worse. Or at least that's what Ellen told herself when she woke to find Mark's side of the bed cold and last night's awful, heavy sensation still pressing on her midriff. As she blinked in the darkness, the memory of their final conversation seemed to bounce off the walls like an echo, with stress making her windpipe burn and her hands tremble. What she couldn't work out was why her body was reacting to his exit with such shock. Hadn't she known that he'd scramble for the door as soon as he discovered the truth?

While other women worried about infidelity, Ellen regarded Google as one of the greatest threats to her happiness, with old newspapers coming a close second. Christ, if anyone should have been used to abrupt endings it was her, but with Mark somehow – she chewed away at her jagged fingernails as she thought about it – she'd imagined that he wouldn't freak out like the others. For the first time in her life she had felt safe, but then the dream imploded after a single, ill-thought-out confession. It was her own stupid fault. After his proposal, she'd told herself it was only fair to tell him that she would never have kids. But why hadn't she just concocted some story about blocked tubes or faulty eggs?

Did she really believe anyone in their right mind would tie themselves to a liability like her, once they knew the full story? Not a chance, she thought, with another angry gnaw at her reddened fingertips. That's why she'd always been careful about contraception, even asking her doctor about sterilisation. The GP had refused, declaring that, at twenty-eight, she was 'too young to make that sort of decision'. But she could see by his wavering gaze that he understood why she wanted it done. Of course he did – he knew her history.

'Whatever it is, nothing will change between us,' Mark had reassured her, when she told him she had something important to say. 'I've never loved anyone the way I love you,' he'd said. A small, hopeful part of her had dared to believe him then, until she saw the doubts bleeding into his face. The next two months passed awkwardly, and it was as if they were stuck in a cold departure lounge waiting for a flight to some far-off place – she knew the parting was coming, she just didn't know when.

'It's you, El,' he'd said last night as he stuffed unfolded clothes into a suitcase. 'Why must you push everyone away? I don't give a monkey's about all that other crap. You're your own worst enemy, you know that?' Fixing his gaze anywhere but on her pale, stricken face, he hadn't even stayed long enough to pack up his beloved rock CDs. *Do you think I'd stick around if I didn't have to?* Ellen had wanted to scream, sorely tempted to hurl one of the Metallica CD cases at the back of his head. Instead she had folded her hands in her lap and sat quietly, with unseen tears rolling down her cheeks.

It was strange to think that she might almost have felt relieved if Mark had run off with someone else – or if not relieved, then at least normal. She'd belong to the same club generations before her had unwittingly joined. After all, there was no shame in being tossed aside for someone richer, sassier or fitter, was there? Why, she could go into work today, wail about Mark's callous disregard and wallow in the kindness of her colleagues; some might even take twisted pleasure in raking over the sordid details and tearing him to shreds. Oh, how she'd love to oblige them.

Her body protested as she trudged to the bathroom, Bow nudging his damp muzzle into her hands as she went. She leaned over and stroked his velvety ears, breaking into a sweat when she straightened up. Massaging her lower back with her knuckles, she groaned as she stepped into the shower, the sad ache in her chest weighing her whole torso down as she washed her hair and then afterwards, standing heavily at the sink to brush her teeth. Bow yawned and sank to the floor, resting his chin on her toes. He looked up at her with a mournful expression, the whites of his eyes visible below a deep molasses brown. With Mark gone, Ellen was worried about the elderly dog being in the house on his own all day. She felt bad for him, but she'd never taken a sickie in her life, and anyway, Bow was going to have to get used to being alone – they both were.

At the thought of the office and the inevitable questions awaiting her, her stomach flipped over again, this time so violently that her ribs actually hurt. Beads of sweat appeared on her forehead and, feeling light-headed, she leaned forward and rested her hands on the cold enamel. She trusted Mark not to tell anyone her secret, but non-committal answers from her would surely leave colleagues puzzled, suspicious even.

Half an hour later, Ellen jogged towards the tram station, the smell of diesel from a passing taxi making her feel sick. Dust swirled up from the street and she turned her face into her coat, gripped by the conviction that, on top of everything else, she was about to come down with a bad dose of flu. She took a deep breath, the icy February air doing nothing to dispel the overwhelming gloom inside her.

If she'd had any real notion of what was about to happen, though, she might have thrown herself under the blasted 7.36 a.m. tram, instead of careering full pelt after it.

'We've started little one on a four-dose course against hepatitis,' the stout midwife, Ciara, whispered as she parked a wheeled metal trolley between the nearby incubator and my chair. It was February 2006, and although I had been registered as a foster carer for almost three years, I had never fostered a newborn before. Captivated by the tiny clothes folded on my lap (pink vests, no bigger than the palm of my hand), it was a moment before I looked up. 'So far she's tested negative,' Ciara continued, glancing around the Special Care Baby Unit to make sure no one was near enough to overhear, 'but without the usual prenatal tests, we've no idea of Mum's status. My guess is that her life-style's been anything but organised.'

Peering around Ciara, all I could see of my new placement was the swirl of downy hair at the crown of her head, but I longed to pick her up and shield her from the harsh overhead lighting, the disinfected air. Lindsey, my supervising social worker at Bright Heights Fostering Agency, had called earlier that morning with a referral from social services – an infant born prematurely two days earlier. The baby girl, temporarily named Hope after the paramedic who delivered her, had stunned everyone with her unexpected arrival, including, so it seemed, her own mother.

'And Mum *really* had no idea she was pregnant?'

Ciara shook her head and pulled on a pair of blue latex gloves. 'No. Well, she was on her way to work when the cramps started, so that shows you how unexpected it was. She collapsed on the tram. It's only when paramedics exam-ined her in the ambulance that they realised what was going on. She didn't *look* pregnant, so they say. We're guessing she was about thirty-four weeks along.' The midwife lowered the side of the incubator, the sing-song tone of her soft Irish lilt even more pronounced as she leaned towards the baby. 'No one on the tram could believe it, could they, dear heart? You surprised everyone, oh yes you did now.'

'Goodness, what a shock,' I said, setting aside the vests and sleep suits and then patting my hands on my lap. By then I was itching for a cuddle.

'Exactly. How d'you get your head round something like that?' She leaned over until her head was level with the base of the transparent crib. 'Ciara just can't imagine how,' she said, moving her head exaggeratedly from side to side. 'Oh no she can't.'

I blew out my cheeks and we shared a baffled look. 'And there's still no word from her?'

Ciara moistened some cotton wool in a pot of water and then spun on clumpy heels so that her face was close to mine. 'The police managed to find her. They called Sister about an hour ago,' she said, her voice low again. 'She's been assessed by a psychiatrist and it seems the shock of the birth has triggered some sort of post-natal post-traumatic stress disorder – I've seen it myself after difficult births. Some women are so traumatised by labour that they find it difficult to form an attachment to the baby. What I can't understand is how she managed to stagger out of here so quickly afterwards.' Ciara shuddered as she straightened. 'Makes your eyes water just thinking about it. Anyway, about the hep B – you'll need to make sure you and your children are protected.'

'Oh dear, that'll please them,' I said with a mock grimace. Inoculation against hepatitis B was one of the requirements of registering as a foster carer, so I was covered, but since my own children were uninvolved in the intimate care of others, our GP had advised that they wouldn't need the vaccination. With a newborn in the house, though, I realised that I might need to reconsider his advice. It was going to be near impossible to keep eleven-year-old Emily and her eight-year-old brother Jamie away from Hope – they adored babies.

Ciara returned her attention to Hope, reaching into the incubator and releasing the tabs of her tiny nappy. Casually rough as only the expertly capable can be, the midwife grasped the infant's ankles between splayed fingers and hoisted them into the air, snatching the soiled nappy away with the other hand. I marvelled at her practised movements as she dabbed Hope's tiny bottom with the pad and then manoeuvred a fresh nappy between an assortment of fine tubes and wires, and I became aware that one of the mothers across the ward had fixed her gaze on me.

The young woman was seated on a rocking chair beside a wide incubator, her twin babies tucked beneath the long baggy jumper she wore. Their identical domed heads were nestled face to face beneath her chin, so still that from across the room she appeared to be cuddling a pair of life-like porcelain dolls. I met her inquisitive gaze with a smile and she asked: 'How's Hope doing today?' I suspected that she was wondering who I was and why the baby beside me had waited so long for her first visitor to arrive.

'She's doing well, I think,' I answered, before tilting my head to indicate her own babies. 'They look comfy there.'

She smiled proudly and resumed her rocking, the slight puzzlement remaining in her eyes as she went slowly to and fro. Hope's sudden appearance had made the local papers, but somehow the hospital had managed to prevent the news of her abandonment being leaked to the press. I wasn't sure how much the midwives had told the other mothers about the case and, as with any foster placement, the details were confidential. Most people were naturally curious and I was still perfecting a polite but firm response whenever anyone asked about children in my care.

'Right, are you ready for her?' Ciara asked, having disposed of the old nappy, removed her gloves and washed her hands.

'Absolutely,' I said with a nervous smile, my stomach performing an excited somersault. It had been a while since I'd held a newborn, especially one as tiny as Hope.

Ciara effortlessly gathered several transparent tubes into a bundle and, clutching them in one hand, scooped Hope up with the other. She set the baby carefully in my waiting arms and covered her with several blankets, tucking them right up to her chin. Hope stirred, her tiny features twisting in protest at the change. Bundling her up in the blankets, I eased her onto my shoulder, careful not to dislodge the fine tube taped to one of her nostrils. Amazed at her kitten-like weight, I rubbed small circular movements over her back with the pads of two fingers, my heart melting as her warmth seeped into my chest.

Straight away she relaxed, her body falling slack against mine. After a few moments I transferred her to the crook of my arm and adjusted the blankets around her, taking in her small features for the first time. Her lashes were almost invisible so that her eyes, closed in a tight line, appeared as fine slits, as if they had been painted on. The skin around them was mottled with faint, uneven patches of blue, her eyebrows barely there. 'She's beautiful,' I whispered to Ciara without glancing up. I liked to think of myself as open-minded enough not to make snap judgements, but at that moment it was difficult to comprehend the wilful abandonment of a helpless baby.

My thoughts began drifting towards her birth mother when the regular, pulsating beeps of the nearby monitor became an insistent wail. 'What is it? What's wrong?' I looked at Ciara with wide eyes.

'It's OK,' she smiled, resetting the alarm with the flick of a switch. 'The monitor's picking up on her altered breathing, that's all. Nothing to worry about.'

I clapped a hand to my chest and let out a breath, struck by the depth of Hope's vulnerability. Suddenly it was scary to think that I would soon assume sole responsibility for her wellbeing. Could the unexpected arrival of someone so fragile be enough to tip a person into some sort of psychosis, I wondered, as I cradled the newborn in my arms.

It wasn't until much later that I began to suspect there was more to Hope's abandonment than any of us realised.

'Ignore the mess,' I said as I led Ellen through the hall. It was Monday of the half-term holidays, and although Hope had been home from hospital for ten days, this was her mother's first contact since she had given birth. I still hadn't cleared away the breakfast things, and there was what could only be described as *stuff* strewn across almost every surface in the living room. Hope's padded changing mat was balanced on top of Emily's giant doll's house, the sofa was littered with Jamie's shin pads and football socks, and the new baby clothes I had ordered online were piled up in the middle of our coffee table, like some way-out arty centrepiece.

'Would you like a cup of tea or something?' I asked, contravening one of the first rules of contact in the foster home. Social workers regularly warned against making home visits too comfortable, as accommodating foster carers sometimes find themselves at the beck and call of demanding birth parents with a penchant for bacon butties and sugary tea.

I'll never forget visits from one young mother, who would mumble a gruff hello as she plodded past me to the sofa, barely glancing in her toddler's direction. Halfway through one session she withdrew a Thermos flask full of chipolata sausages from her mucky rucksack and proceeded to chomp on them two at a time, head tilted backwards for faster swallowing.

Grudgingly impressed that she'd bothered to cook her own snacks (neglecting to provide food was one of the reasons her little one had been removed from home), I commented on her resourcefulness. 'S'easy,' she shrugged, still dressed in pyjamas; she didn't seem to feel it necessary to dress before leaving the house. 'Marks do bangers ready cooked. I just stick 'em in the zinger for a couple a secs and that's it. Done.'

Unable to resist, I asked her if her son liked them as well. 'Oh, God, I don't give 'em to him. He eats them frankfurter thingies that come in a jar. Has 'em cold. I wouldn't eat that crap, personally,' she'd added with a righteous shudder. What had surprised me most of all, though, was her reply when her toddler asked to participate in her feast. 'Na,' she'd said, shooing him away with greasy fingers. 'Ask Rosie for summat.'

In Ellen's case I couldn't help myself, though. Her skin was as white as paper and there was a bluish tinge around her chapped lips – a telltale sign that she'd been walking around in the cold for a long time, perhaps trying to summon the courage to visit. It may have been instinct, or the glint of terror in her eyes, but something told me she needed a minute or two to gather herself before being reunited with her baby.

The picture of her floating around in my mind over the past week had been way off beam. I had imagined a frame heavy enough to disguise a pregnancy, along with hardened features and an impassive, callous nature. In the flesh, Ellen was of small build, wiry even, in her slim-fitting jeans and cable-knit jumper. She had a pleasant face, although a pained expression tightened her small features. I almost wanted to reach out and give her a hug.

There was no visible sign of her recent pregnancy either, not even a hint of the stubborn mummy tummy that still stalked me eight years after leaving the labour ward. I had heard of surprise births before, but with Ellen's build it was almost impossible to believe that she hadn't known she was pregnant, unless of course she had wilfully chosen to ignore it – it was amazing what people were capable of overlooking, if they truly wanted to.

'No,' she snapped in reply to my offer of tea, before adding a gentler, 'I'm fine, thank you.' Standing in the middle of the room, she was frowning at the floor, as if for a moment she'd forgotten why she was here.

'OK, well, make yourself comfortable,' I said, nodding towards the sofa. 'If you can find a space,' I added with a laugh. I sat next to her and chattered on for a few minutes, but, distracted by Hope's soft, contented coos, her eyes kept straying over to the Moses basket. 'I've been trying to have a sort-out but ...' My sentence trailed off as I crossed the room and leaned over the crib. 'Here's the cause of all the trouble,' I said, picking up Hope and kneeling in front of Ellen.

Ellen paused and then said, 'Oh, yes, yes,' her eyes flicking over her daughter. Before looking away she added, 'She's very small,' almost as if she felt the occasion shouldn't pass without comment and she couldn't think of anything else to say.

'Yes, it's like holding fresh air,' I said, rising to my feet.

Perhaps sensing that I was about to hand the baby to her, Ellen snatched up her bag with a look of alarm. 'I've got a card for her in here somewhere,' she said, rummaging around exaggeratedly. 'The social worker said I should write one for her memory box.'

I studied her for a second or two and then took the proffered card, but not before I'd noticed it vibrating in her trembling fingers. 'That's nice, thank you,' I said, transferring Hope to my shoulder. With a steadying hand on her back, I set the card on top of one of the piles of small clothes and then sat at the other end of the sofa.

Ellen lowered her bag to the floor, bloodshot eyes flitting nervously around the room. 'Is there anything I can do to help?' she asked, with a note of desperation.

At that moment I remembered reading somewhere that accepting a favour from someone was one of the best ways of helping them to feel at ease. I had always found that asking children for help, even ones with severe behavioural difficulties, worked like magic, and so I immediately accepted Ellen's offer, indicating the small clothes in front of her with a nod of my head. 'I was about to go through those, cut the labels out and then put away the ones that won't fit her yet.'

She grabbed a pair of scissors and got to work immediately, seeming relieved to have a task to do. 'So, how are you feeling?' I asked after a few moments, trying to get a conversation going and perhaps help her to relax.

Unfortunately, my question had the opposite effect. The scissors froze in her hand and her jaw stiffened. For a moment she looked so tense that I glanced away. When I looked back I said, even more softly, 'It must have been such a shock.' She bit her lip thoughtfully and nodded, eyes downcast.

'Well, Hope's emerged pretty unscathed,' I continued in a brighter tone, stroking her cheek with the edge of my finger. 'I expect you've heard that's what we're calling her, until you've decided on a name.'

She looked up, seemingly confused. After a pause she shrugged, discarding one of the labels from a small vest. 'Hope seems as good a name as any,' she said, twisting her knees around so that she was angled away, somehow in the room but not really with us. It was sad to see her so distanced from her own baby, where even choosing a name seemed to be an intimacy she preferred to avoid. And yet there had been a flicker of something in her expression when she had first glanced at Hope – a wisp of tenderness, perhaps; longing, even. In other circumstances I might have passed the baby to her and then pottered nearby but, sensing her nerves, I decided to hold back. I couldn't see any point in forcing the issue and, from the way Ellen's eyes darted nervously back and forth every time Hope stirred, it was almost as if she was frightened of her own baby.

'It is a nice name, suits her somehow,' I said, wittering on as Ellen worked. I told her about Hope's routine, or more precisely, her lack of one. Despite her time in the SCBU, where the midwives stuck to a well-practised routine, her days and nights were still mixed up. 'My Emily was the same,' I said with a muffled yawn, 'but for the life of me I can't remember what I did about it.' I threw her a one-sided smile and she responded with a weak noise of polite amusement, her eyes every so often skimming the sleeping baby. There was a glimmer of interest – I was sure of it.

'Mind you,' I continued, brushing feathery wisps of dark hair back from Hope's brow, 'I didn't know anyone else but my mum to ask for tips when I first had Emily, and she could barely remember having little ones. Emily was born the day after I went on maternity leave so I didn't get a chance to meet any other mums until after she was born. And when I did I felt so out of it, like I didn't belong. I just didn't feel like one of them, you know? It was all a bit overwhelming.'

Ellen paused and then returned her attention to snipping the labels off.

'Are there any babies in your family? Any nieces or nephews?'

'There's no one,' she replied stiffly, folding the last of the sleep suits and shoving her hands between her knees. She sat still, eyelids flickering, and then snatched her bag up, catching it by the front flap. The clasp opened with a small popping noise, and receipts, a stick of lip balm and a small black purse spilled out onto the floor. For a moment she looked as if she might burst into tears, but instead she let out a huff of exasperation. 'I've only got half an hour today,' she snapped, ramming her purse back into her bag and closing her fingers around the clasp.

To her credit, Ellen turned up on time for every contact, even one day when heavy snow had caused travel chaos across the whole of northern England. Since Hope was very young, Ellen was entitled to five two-hour sessions a week, although her social worker had told me in a hurried telephone conversation that the looked-after children's team manager was already considering a reduction.

The problem was that, two weeks after her first visit, Ellen was still showing minimal interest in her baby. With the awkwardness of the first meeting over and done with, she found a place easily among us, as I sensed she would. She relaxed enough to chat about day-to-day things, and I felt comfortable in her company. We managed to get a bit of a rapport going but still, both of us continued to tiptoe around the elephant in the room – her avoidance of Hope. She began to open up about other things, telling me that she was still adjusting to being alone after the end of a serious relationship. When I sympathised she almost bit my head off, telling me it was 'just one of those things', but the weepy expression on her face belied her shrugs.

Despite her snappiness and tendency for gloom (if she dropped something, her automatic reaction was to groan and pronounce it 'Typical!'), she was a straightforward character and fundamentally I liked her. Whenever she was around she busied herself with sterilising and making up bottles, washing Hope's vests and sleep suits and generally making herself useful, but if I so much as suggested any sort of hands-on care she lost what little colour she had and raced off to the bathroom.

What I couldn't work out was why she continued to visit so diligently, if she had no intention of caring for Hope herself. It was as if being around her daughter and dealing with the practicalities was enough for her, and I wondered if perhaps she was afraid of getting too close. She didn't strike me as the sort of person who would abdicate responsibility easily – she told me how hard she'd worked after leaving school, making her way up the ladder and securing a responsible office job – and if it was fear holding her back, I wanted to help her, or at least know that I had tried.

Whatever the truth of it, I knew the situation couldn't continue. Understandably, social services were keen to reach a swift decision on Hope's future, and whenever Graham Thorpe, Hope's social worker, called for an update, he sounded none too impressed with the lack of progress. I felt a little guilty as I reported Ellen's reluctance to bond with her daughter – almost as if I was betraying her – but it would have been irresponsible of me to skew the facts, however much I had come to like Ellen. Graham confided that she had been invited to attend counselling sessions but had so far declined, something she hadn't mentioned to me. Refusing to engage was another black mark against her and would do nothing to improve her chances of keeping her baby, if she even wanted to – it was difficult to tell.

Remembering what Ciara, one of the midwives, had said about post-natal post-traumatic stress disorder, I rose early one morning and researched the condition on the internet. I already knew a little about it, as a police officer friend of mine who had been involved in helping victims of the 7/7 bombings was still suffering terrible nightmares months later, and I had heard of soldiers suffering in the same way after being in war zones. Until Ciara mentioned it, though, I had never heard of childbirth being a potential trigger.

According to a number of websites, anyone could develop post-traumatic stress disorder (PTSD) after a period of intense fear or shock. Often, sufferers seek to avoid anything that could remind them of the traumatic event, so victims of the terrorist attacks in London might steer clear of public transport. Sadly, women who suffer extreme distress as a result of a difficult labour sometimes seek to avoid the biggest reminder of the ordeal – their own baby.

In a society where birth and newborns are romanticised, a woman in such a situation might feel even more isolated, especially when the potent cocktail of wildly fluctuating hormones is added to the mix. While Ellen's labour may not have been traumatic in a physical sense, I guessed that giving birth unexpectedly might have had a massive psychological impact.

Post-natal PTSD certainly might explain her closed-down expression whenever she glanced at Hope, conflicting emotions perhaps leaving her frozen. But I suspected that there was more to her distance than that. One site I came across detailed some heartbreaking case studies of new mums who had felt so overwhelmed by panic that they ended their lives, too terrified to reach out for help through fear of being judged. Many of them had no close relatives to turn to for support, and as I read about them I thought of Ellen's caginess whenever our conversation drifted towards family. As far as I could make out, apart from work colleagues there was no one close to her; no mother, father or even siblings.

Interestingly, one site I clicked on suggested that previous traumas were sometimes reignited by childbirth, and that it wasn't unusual for mothers (and fathers) who had been adopted or fostered as children to start experiencing flashbacks to their early lives after having a child of their own. A psychologist went on to explain that if a woman had been sexually abused during childhood, the loss of control experienced during labour sometimes proved to be a potent reminder of her own powerlessness. The let-down reflex and physical sensations associated with breastfeeding also sometimes resurrected painful memories that had long since been buried. The thought that the momentous experience of childbirth could be overshadowed in such a way filled me with sadness and really got me thinking. As the days passed I became more and more convinced that Ellen was guarding more than just her own emotions.

Halfway through her third week of contact, when Hope was about five weeks old, I presented her with an album of photos chronicling her baby's days since birth. It was something I did for all the children I looked after, although when they were older I kept a weekly rather than daily record. She stared at me for a long time, seemingly astounded, as if she'd never been given a present before. 'It's nothing much,' I said, waving my hand through the air as she opened the cover and slowly, reverentially turned the pages. 'Just a little something to ...' I broke off at the sound of a small cry from Hope. Ellen looked up sharply, her hand frozen in mid-air.

Looking past me to where her baby was resting on a soft blanket spread out over a rug in front of the fireplace, her brow crumpled. My eyes followed hers just as Hope's cries began to escalate into tiny screams. With some difficulty I restrained myself from going to her, compelling Ellen to comfort her instead. 'I think she's hungry,' I said, gently prompting. And then, turning towards the kitchen, I said, 'I'll get her bottle ready.'

She caught me by the forearm, her grip tight and frantic. 'No,' she almost snarled, her eyes spinning from Hope to me and back again. Her hair was beginning to slip out of her ponytail and she looked very young and vulnerable. 'I'll get it for you,' she said, a little more gently, and from her panicked expression I could tell that she found her baby's cries unbearable. At the same time, she couldn't bring herself to do anything about them.

After settling Hope into her crib for a sleep half an hour later, Ellen handed me a cup of steaming tea. She was looking at me carefully, and a moment later she sucked in a breath as if readying herself to say something. I felt my pulse quicken, but before she could get any words out the telephone rang. 'It's probably someone selling something,' I said, with a little shrug of my shoulders. I was ready to ignore it but when the shrill tone finally stopped I knew the moment was lost; Ellen had turned away and was folding one of the small cardigans my mother had knitted for Hope. Cupping the mug of tea in my hands, I stood staring at Ellen's back, but when the insistent ring started up again, I answered it after only a moment's hesitation.

It was Graham, Hope's social worker. 'How's it going?' he asked. We hadn't spoken for a couple of days but I knew he was in the process of compiling a report for the interim court hearing. Without positive feedback, he was likely to proceed with a request for a reduction in contact. 'Erm, OK. Ellen's here at the moment. Can we talk later?'

'No can do, I'm afraid, Rosie. I really need to finish this report and I'm tied up in meetings for the rest of the day.'

Cupping my hand over the mouthpiece, I whispered to Ellen's back, 'Sorry, I'll nip in the other room to take this.' Feeling faintly embarrassed since there was only a wall separating us, I told Graham that there wasn't much to report.

'She still hasn't even picked the baby up?'

'Um, no,' I said hesitantly, 'but I get the feeling she wants to. Something's holding her back.'

'Yes,' Graham said heavily. 'She's a very troubled girl. The sooner we get Hope sorted the better.'

My jaw grew tight, knowing that Graham was talking about adoption. Despite a strong desire for Hope to settle into permanence as quickly as possible, I couldn't help feeling sad knowing it probably meant lifelong separation from Ellen. 'Graham, I really think that with support –'

'Rosie,' he interrupted sharply, 'Ellen's making no effort to bond with Hope. I'm not feeling optimistic at all, especially not with her past. No, I'm afraid it's all looking a bit grim.'

Nettled, I didn't take everything he said in. 'It's been less than three weeks,' I said with a slight coolness, 'I don't think –'

'Look, to be frank, Rosie, you're not paid to think.'

145

I caught my breath and said nothing, his words about Ellen's past beginning to register. After a moment he seemed to realise he'd been a bit sharp and rushed to cover himself. 'What I mean is, leave us to worry about the care plan. Ellen can't go swanning in and out of the child's life whenever she feels like it and not even lift a finger to care for her. You're doing an excellent job with young Hope so just carry on doing what you're doing and I'll keep you informed. I'm sure we both want to secure a positive outcome for her.'

Annoyed, I made a noise of assent but said little else. Graham still hadn't visited personally to check on Hope, sending an agency social worker as stand-in on his behalf. I knew how overwhelmed the local authority staff were and so had no complaint about that, but since we hadn't even met, his praise came across as a little false. Being slapped down for offering an opinion was irritating as well, but the wishes and feelings of foster carers were often disregarded, so I was used to that. It was fair enough in some ways – I was *just* a foster carer with no official qualification in social work, but I had spent more time in Ellen's company than any other professional. Surely that should count for something? What had really annoyed me, though, was Graham's attitude towards Ellen, when he barely knew her. She couldn't hear what was being said, but I minded on her behalf.

'If she'll relinquish Hope and agree to the adoption, things will run a lot more smoothly,' Graham continued. He was speaking quickly, clearly in a rush. 'We have several couples on our books waiting for a white British baby and countless others further afield. What I need you to do, Rosie, is record absolutely everything. If Ellen contests our decision your diaries may be summoned by the court.'

The next day, as soon as Ellen took her coat off and sat on the sofa, I was beside her, Hope wrapped in a blanket in my arms. 'Ellen,' I said, my tone serious. She turned her head and looked at me quizzically. 'It's time, love.'

'Time?' Her expression grew wary. 'For what?'

'To take a risk.'

She stopped cold, her eyes falling to her sleeping daughter. Shifting so that my knees were close to hers, I leaned towards her but, startled and panicky, she kept her hands frozen in her lap. At that moment the phone rang and my heart leapt with gratitude; the timing couldn't have been more perfect. 'I have to get that,' I said in a rush, making a snap decision. Standing abruptly, I planted poor Hope unceremoniously onto her mother's lap.

Ellen's eyes widened with alarm, but instinctively she closed her arms around her daughter. As soon as I was confident that Hope was secure I whisked my hands away and rushed off to the kitchen to answer the phone. It was one of those annoying recorded announcements, as it happened, but rather deviously I stayed in the kitchen, bustling around with the phone fixed to my ear. Downstairs, our house is open plan; as I pulled damp clothes from the washing machine and draped them one-handed over the radiators I kept my eyes trained on Ellen. She was cradling

Hope as tenderly as any new mother and, touched, I felt a jolt of optimism at the sight, hopeful that some time alone without the pressure of someone watching might help Ellen to relax and build the confidence she needed to start caring for her daughter. When I returned about ten minutes later, though, she looked up at me with tears in her eyes. 'I don't know what to do. I don't even know how to hold her.'

I knelt in front of her and touched a thumb to Hope's forehead. 'But you are holding her, my love.'

'No, no, I'm not. Not properly. I don't know where to put myself to make her comfortable. My arm's digging in the back of her head.'

I laughed under my breath. 'She looks happy enough to me.' It was true. Hope was staring up at her mother's face with solemn intrigue, her tiny fingers moving fluidly through the air between them. Every so often she interlaced them like an elderly professor, quietly assessing this new situation.

'I don't know anything about looking after a baby,' Ellen said in shallow, jerky breaths. 'I haven't got a clue what to do if she cries or throws up or anything.'

I scoffed. 'You learn quickly when a baby's involved, believe me. They don't give you any choice.'

'How? How will I learn?'

'You'll learn together. Hope will let you know what she needs.'

Ellen let out a frustrated breath. 'You make it sound so easy.'

I gave her a pacifying smile and shook my head. 'I don't mean to. It's the most natural thing in the world and the hardest, all at the same time. You'll gradually get to know what to do when she cries or if she won't go to sleep. But I tell you something. Whatever happens, and wherever she goes, you'll never learn to stop loving her.' I shook my head. 'No, you'll never be able to do that.'

Ellen jerked her head up sharply. She was frowning and I gave her a direct look. 'Perhaps you haven't recognised it yet, or maybe it's so scary that you can't even begin to, but I can see it, even if you can't.'

'See it? What do you mean?'

'You're smitten, Ellen. It's written all over your face.'

Before I'd even finished my sentence Ellen gave a loud sob, and Hope's arms splayed out in shock, her bottom lip trembling. She stared up at Ellen with wide eyes, her lips rolled in on themselves, her face turning crimson from holding her breath. 'There, it's all right,' I said soothingly, slipping my hands beneath her arms and twisting her carefully away from Ellen onto my shoulder. Rubbing small circles on her back to encourage her to breathe, I could feel her tense body slowly unwinding and then she bawled, the screams coming in short bursts between sharp, panicky breaths. Eventually, they slowed until she was mewing like a kitten, her face wet with real tears. 'That's better, shhh,' I crooned, twisting my head to look at Ellen as I moved from one foot to the other. She was crying into her hands, shoulders trembling.

'Ellen?' I said softly, after calming Hope and settling

her in her crib. Ellen continued to sob, hands still covering her face. I sat beside her and waited quietly. After a minute or so she lowered her hands and sniffed, apologising. 'Don't,' I said, handing her a tissue. 'You don't have to apologise.'

She jutted out her chin and blew air up on her face until her fringe fluttered. At that moment there was a heavy clomping on the stairs and then Emily and Jamie appeared in the open doorway, their bright smiles fading when I raised my eyebrows and made a face at them. Emily backed from the room, dragging Jamie by the jumper. 'Hey! Get off! I want to cuddle Hope,' I heard Jamie shout before Emily closed the door discretely behind them.

A scuffle ensued in the hall but Ellen didn't seem to notice. After blowing her nose she rolled the tissue up into a ball and shoved her hands between her knees, looking up at the ceiling. I watched her without saying anything, waiting for the power of silence to do its work. 'I'm not a nice person,' she said, after what felt like an age.

An unexpected chill ran across my scalp, Graham's words about Ellen being troubled coming back to me in a rush. However much I felt I had the measure of her, foster carers took a risk when opening up their homes to birth parents. The truth was, I had no idea what he'd been referring to when he mentioned her past; I barely knew anything about her at all. I rubbed a hand across the back of my neck and took a steadying breath. 'Why do you say that?'

She groaned and leaned forward, forearms touching her knees, hands cupping her face. 'Because I'm not.'

Unexpected

I pursed my lips and shook my head. 'Sorry, I don't see that at all.'

She let out a frustrated breath. 'You don't know anything about me, Rosie.'

I paused, considering. 'I know enough. I know you're considerate and kind and warm.'

'How can you say that?' she scoffed, sounding angry. 'I walked out on my own baby. What sort of person does that?'

I thought about it and answered gently. 'A very frightened one, I'd say.'

She spun around to face me. 'No, you're wrong,' she snapped, her eyes flashing black. 'Most women would do anything to protect their babies, no matter how scared they are. Even animals know how to do that – I read something once, about female gazelles. Did you know that they walk away from their young as soon as they're born?' I shook my head but Ellen didn't notice; she was staring at her hands as she knotted them over and over in her lap. 'People used to think they were cold, reckless animals until someone realised that what they were doing was diverting the attention of predators away from their babies and onto themselves. *That's* normal. It's what most people do. What I did was unnatural. There's something wrong with me. I'm like my mother. She should never have had children and neither should I.'

I nodded slowly, aware that Ellen had stilled and was watching me intently, trying to gauge my reaction. As I considered a reply, my mind flashed back to the child psychology books I'd read when registering as a foster carer. How someone responded to disclosures mattered; tone, pitch and posture all worked together to either encourage or deter the child from continuing. Something as simple as a minute shrug or a raised eyebrow had the power to undermine the child's trust, perhaps deterring them from ever disclosing anything again. Instinct told me that talking to adults wasn't too far different, and so I waited a few seconds, mentally rehearsing my voice until it was neutral, and then said, 'I think you'd make a wonderful mother, Ellen, if only you'd give yourself that chance.'

A spasm of pain passed over her face. 'You sound just like Mark,' she said, looking up at the ceiling with a mixture of scorn and exasperation.

I looked up sharply. I knew that Mark was her ex-fiancé and had walked out on her, but I had no idea there had been any contact between them. 'He knows about Hope?' I asked, surprised. She stood abruptly and began pacing the room. 'Ellen?'

'Yes, he knows,' she snapped. 'Social services insisted he has rights. They told him yesterday and now he won't stop calling me.'

I frowned. She hadn't confided much about him, but I was under the impression that she had been heartbroken over the break-up. 'Does he want to see her? Is that why he –'

'He says it was my fault we ended, that I kept pushing him away until he had no choice but to leave.'

I considered that for a moment. 'And what do you think?'

She stopped pacing for a moment and shrugged. 'I suppose he's right. I've done it all my life. But now he wants to get back together and play happy families.'

'And you don't?'

She closed her eyes and tipped her head back in frustration. 'I've told you, Rosie, I'm *not* normal. It could never work. He's better off without me.'

'And Hope is too?'

She sighed contemptuously and began pacing again. I let a few seconds pass and then said, 'Presumably Mark knows you well?'

She scoffed. 'Mark thinks he can make everything better. He says love's a cure for everything.'

'Well, I'd agree with him there.'

She shook her head and narrowed her eyes, tuning me out. Continually moving, she paused between each step as if her thoughts were weighing so heavily that she was fearful she might step through the floor. Every so often she looked over at me and I got the sense that she wanted to open up, but she just couldn't find the words to begin. Eventually I invited her to join me in the kitchen, where I switched the kettle on. I emptied the teapot, swirled tap water around the inside and filled it with boiling water, adding two teabags before replacing the lid.

Sitting on a high stool, I rested my mug of tea on my lap and stared at the rising steam. Ellen continued to pace, biting her lip as she went. I had the feeling she was close to opening up because as I stared at my drink I could feel her eyes on me. Finally, she started to talk. 'I've tried so hard to forget,' she said in a low monotone, her voice sounding as if it was coming from far away. 'But since,' she inclined her head towards the living room, where Hope was now sleeping peacefully, 'since last month, I can't seem to get it out of my mind. What happened when – when –' she stumbled over her words, licking her lips as she grappled for the right way to express herself. 'When –'

'When you were little?' I suggested, not daring to move. I didn't want anything to put her off continuing.

She shot me a look and then pressed a hand to her mouth. 'All that hurt,' she said, shivering. She wrapped her arms around herself. 'I've tried so hard to put it all behind me. When I met Mark I thought I'd finally overcome the past. But it never goes away, no matter how badly you want it to. It seeps into everything, ripping and tearing it up. I don't want that for Hope. She has a chance to escape that sort of life – how can I take that away from her?'

'Your mother, you said?' I asked, carefully avoiding her question with one of my own. She nodded and began to shake uncontrollably. It was difficult to watch and I felt sorry for pressing her then, but at the same time I knew that something had to give. I had pussyfooted around her fear of Hope for weeks and it hadn't helped either of them. Silence might be less painful for both of us, but it would resolve nothing. 'What happened, Ellen?' I prompted gently.

Her eyelids flickered as she looked over at me, and I could see she was struggling to express herself. 'She was brutal,' she managed to say, blinking away the tears. 'From as early as I can remember I was petrified of her. You never knew, you see, what mood she'd be in when you got up. One day she'd be OK and you'd start to relax, but the next she'd drag you by the hair and starve you.'

I nodded as she spoke in what I hoped was an encouraging way, and I was struck by the way she distanced herself from her story by referring to herself in the second person rather than the first. Ellen opened her mouth and closed it again. My heart filled with sorrow for her. 'That must have been very hard, not feeling safe.' It was one of the first things I told children as soon as they arrived in placement – 'You're safe now.' For many, these words came as such a relief.

She dabbed her nose on her sleeve and nodded. 'I still don't know why she was like she was. All I know is that she didn't love me, didn't even like me, actually.' Tears rolled down her cheeks as she continued, her voice reedy with emotion. 'Do you know what my earliest memory is?'

I pressed my lips together and shook my head, restraining myself from standing up and putting an arm around her. 'I'm sitting on the floor in the kitchen, stacking tins or whatever it is that toddlers do. My mother walks in and I smile up at her. We'd had a few good days and I'd almost forgotten what she could be like. I adored her.' Ellen faltered and then cleared her throat. 'But then I notice that look on her face she gets sometimes and I start to cry because I know what's coming, but still I put my arms up to her when she comes over because I think maybe there's a chance that she'll be nice to me. I think that maybe if I look at her and show her how much I love her she'll pick me up and comfort me. Do you know what she does then? She kicks me in the face. No warning, no build-up, nothing. She just kicks me in the face and then stands over me, screaming, 'You disgust me, Ellen. You're a disgusting, horrible child.'

Ellen looked at me, tears rolling down her cheeks. 'Her words are still here,' she wept, jabbing her forefinger into her temple until the skin whitened around it. 'Everything she did and said reminded me that I was a complete failure, and that never goes away, no matter how hard you try to forget. God, no wonder I never realised I was pregnant. I'd been carrying that weight around inside me ever since I could walk. Do you know what the strange thing is, though? I still long for her, almost every day. When I was in A&E with Hope, all I wanted was my mum. How screwed up am I?'

'Oh, Ellen,' I said, on the verge of tears myself, 'that's not strange at all.' So many of the children I had looked after spent their days pining for the love of a mother who was sealed off from them; one that never had existed and probably never would. Hungry for affection, it was so hard for them to accept that they wouldn't ever have access to the source of comfort so many others took for granted.

Such callous abuse cut me to the core, and a hot feeling of anger pressed on my breastbone as I thought about the parents who abused their own offspring to fulfil their own needs. I could see how Ellen's past had led her to believe she was unlovable, so much so that she ended up pushing anyone close to her away, but I had seen youngsters resist and move on from that sort of cruelty. 'Lots of people learn from their parents' mistakes, Ellen,' I said quietly. 'They know how bad it feels to live like that, so they do the opposite. Having your own child is like being given a second chance.'

Staring at the floor, she bit her lip, eyes darting rapidly to and fro. 'But what if I can't?' she cried. 'Sometimes I feel so angry. What if I end up being just like her? I can't take that risk with Hope. I want someone to sing her lullabies and rock her to sleep, to read her bedtime stories and tuck her in at night, to have all the things I never had.'

I placed my hand, palm down, on the worktop. 'Exactly,' I said with a meaningful look. 'And you can give her all those things. You're not your mother, Ellen. You've made a conscious choice not to be like her. That means that Hope will be safe with you.'

We talked until the light outside faded and the air around us cooled. I drew the curtains, lit the lamps and began stacking logs in the grate. Hope stirred, surprising us both with a loud, adorable yawn as I lit the kindling. Waiting to be picked up, she fidgeted, making sweet little noises as she sucked on her fist. Ellen gathered up her things while the bottle was warming, and as she passed me on her way to the hall I placed my hand on her arm. 'Thank you for trusting me, Ellen,' I said quietly.

She gave me a tearful, grateful nod in return. 'Don't worry. I'll be all right,' she said, before letting herself out, perhaps quietly counselling herself as well as trying to reassure me.

Emily and Jamie charged downstairs at the sound of the front door closing. To make up for missing out on an earlier cuddle, I told Jamie he could give Hope her bottle. Grinning widely as he sat on the sofa, he cradled her carefully in attentive arms. I sat beside him as she fed, my conversation with Ellen replaying itself in my mind. It seemed that the shock of giving birth to Hope had released the demons of Ellen's own childhood, ones that she had tried very hard to lock away. Now, it was as if she was trapped between two lives – the one carved out for her by a callous parent, and the peaceful, happy one she craved. Affected by what I'd heard, I was desperate to help her find a way to move on.

When Ellen arrived for her next contact with Hope she was withdrawn, something I had anticipated after our heart to heart the day before. Hope was in her sixth week but still had her days and nights mixed up, and she slept heavily as I made us some tea. When she eventually whimpered I re-boiled the kettle and dropped her bottle into a jug, handing the milk to Ellen without comment when it was warm enough.

My heart soared as she lifted the drowsy baby from her crib, and I couldn't resist peering in at the pair of them from the kitchen. Hope sucked without fully waking, her hands flexing and relaxing as she drank. Ellen's eyes never left her daughter's face, tears rolling down her cheeks as she sang softly under her breath and rocked her gently to and fro. My heart went out to her, my own eyes misting at the sight.

The moment seemed to be a turning point for Ellen. From then on, whenever she arrived for contact she went straight to Hope and picked her up, cradling her if she was asleep, playing with her during her lengthening wakeful periods. One afternoon towards the end of March, when Hope was six weeks old, Ellen rested her on a blanket on the floor. Hope lay still for a few minutes, thin legs bowed beneath her nappy, but, having recently woken from a long sleep, she grew livelier with each passing second, her grey-blue eyes flicking from her mother's face to the ceiling and back again. Leaning forward at the waist, Ellen began making soft cooing noises. Hope caught her breath and stilled, watching her mother intently. Concentrating hard, her eyes were wide, her tongue darting between intrigued lips. The next second, her mouth opened in a silent laugh, her eyes lighting up with a fleeting twinkle. Ellen shot me a look of amazement. 'Was that –?'

'Her first smile? Yes, I think it was!' I said, laughing.

Ellen made a noise of disbelief, a sort of half laugh, half cry. Scooping Hope up, she closed her eyes and clutched her baby to her chest.

The weeks of early spring passed rapidly, with Ellen taking over care of Hope whenever she was around. She spoke to her baby almost constantly, reading about ways to stimulate and encourage her development when Hope slept. With her confidence burgeoning, her careful attentiveness turned playful and she would nuzzle Hope's neck with her chin or blow raspberries on her tummy, her baby convulsing with breathless giggles as she gripped her mother's hair. It was like watching someone reinvent themselves before my eyes, and I couldn't have been happier to witness it.

It was during one of our quiet moments together, as we sat reading, that Ellen told me a bit more about her family. From the way she had described her past, I imagined her as an only child of a single mother, when in fact her parents had stayed together until her father passed away when Ellen was in her early twenties. According to Ellen, her father had been a distant man who often worked away, and it was during his long absences that her mother was most abusive. While Ellen had been singled out for her worst punishments, her elder sister appeared to be well treated, something that compounded the hurt. It came as a huge shock to Ellen when, as a teenager, her elder sister accused her father of molesting her throughout her childhood.

Her father was sent to prison and, sickeningly, her mother stood by him and disowned her eldest daughter. With parole, Ellen's father served just over two years, and on release his wife accepted him back into the family home with open arms. Since the case made all the local newspapers at the time and there was much speculation as to whether her father had abused other young children, Ellen felt her family was notorious, particularly as they found themselves targeted by vigilantes. As soon as she was old enough Ellen fled the area, and she still had no idea of her sister's whereabouts – unsure if she was even still alive.

As I listened to her story a wave of fury swept over me, although I felt calmer when she told me that she had returned to confront her mother after her father's death. Her mother refused to acknowledge any mistreatment, as abusers often do, but she had been unable to meet Ellen's gaze, and knowing that she had been challenged satisfied my thirst for justice.

I made sure I updated Graham, the social worker, regularly with positive reports of Ellen and Hope's growing bond, careful not to exaggerate her progress in case he should think that I was overstepping the mark. My calls were met with a sort of impassive lethargy and I began to fear that Hope's future had already been decided, especially when Graham recalled Ellen for a second psychiatric evaluation.

Ellen had been so relieved when she told me that she had passed an initial assessment, and she was bemused when the local authority ordered a second opinion. I had heard of social workers requesting repeated assessments of birth parents from different psychiatrists until their professional conclusion matched that of social services, and so, although I tried to reassure Ellen, I was secretly afraid that things weren't going her way.

In mid-April, when Hope was two months old, Ellen was summoned to the local authority offices for a meeting with Graham and his team manager. I wanted to believe that everything would work out for her, but it was

impossible to second guess their care plan, and when I saw
Ellen later that same day it was instantly clear that it was
not good news.

'They're parallel planning,' she sobbed as she walked up
the wet path towards me. The rain had been relentless since
dawn, the spiralling ribbons of water coursing over her feet
and turning the small pile of fallen leaves at the end of the
path into a sludgy mess. Standing aside to let her in, I
squeezed her arm as she walked past me into the living room.

'I'm pretty sure that's standard procedure,' I said consol-
ingly as I sat on a nearby armchair. Parallel planning meant
that social workers were investigating a number of options
for Hope's future. It was a way of ensuring that there was
no delay in securing permanency for a child. 'Just in case
things don't work out as planned.'

'No, but that's the thing,' she choked tearfully. 'They
don't want me to have her – I could tell. Graham made it
obvious. He said that they have lots of wonderful couples
who are desperate for a healthy baby like Hope. He said
they have concerns because I've been depressed in the past
and, well, you know what sort of childhood I had.'

'What about Mark? Hasn't he shown an interest?'

'He's asked to be assessed but he works long hours and
doesn't have much of a support network. They've said they
don't think he'll cope on his own.' She glanced towards the
crib where Hope was sleeping. 'I love her so much, Rosie.
When Graham said they might take her away for good I
was frantic. Whenever I leave here all I can think about is
being near her again. The thought of her going away for

good, somewhere I can't hold her …' She shook her head. 'I don't think I could bear it,' she said, swallowing hard. 'But maybe Graham's right. I'm on my own and I have to work. I've tried to picture myself being one of those mums who's brilliant at juggling it all but it's like trying to grab hold of thin air because I have nothing to base it on. The couples Graham was talking about are all professional people with plenty of money and lovely houses. If she's adopted, they could give her everything.'

I gave her a sceptical look. 'Maybe they can. I've known brilliant adopters, and I'm sure whomever she went to would love her like she's their own. But you can do that too. A big house and plenty of money doesn't mean much to a baby, Ellen. If you truly want to, you can give her everything she needs.'

'I do want her, with all my heart.'

'Then you must fight for her,' I said. Plenty of the abusive parents I had met were vocal in shouting their love for their children from the rooftops, but it rarely translated into action. Sometimes, all social workers wanted to see from parents was a commitment to doing the best for their children.

'I don't think I'm strong enough,' Ellen said huskily, tears spilling freely from her eyes.

I got up and sat next to her, taking one of her hands in mine. It was small and warm and trembling. 'You're going to have to be, darling,' I said, with a firm nod of my head. 'If you want to keep her, you're going to have to be strong. And if you want me to, I'll help you every step of the way.'

She took a breath. 'But I'm on my own. My life's not set up the way those adopters' lives are. I have no family and no security. All I have is my job, a tiny flat and a huge mortgage. Oh, and a depressed dog who's left on his own all day. I don't know how a baby could possibly fit in to all of that.'

I smiled. 'You'll find a place for her, if you look hard enough.'

Another week passed with no word from Graham or anyone else at social services. Increasingly desperate for a positive decision, Ellen rang them every day, even sitting outside Graham's office for hours at a time, trying to prove to him that she was determined to take care of her daughter. She kept telling me that no news had to be good news but, personally, I wasn't as confident. The decisions of social workers, like the verdicts of juries, were sometimes unfathomable and impossible to predict.

Hope was a joy to care for. At ten weeks, she was already making a series of different sounds in response to Ellen's chatter, and her babble held us all enchanted, Emily and Jamie in particular. Irresistibly drawn to her, they tended to pick Hope up for a hug whenever the mood took them. Since Ellen only got two hours a day with her daughter, I had worried that she might resent their interest, but she seemed to delight in it, calling them over whenever Hope did something she thought they might like. A strange rattling gurgle in Hope's throat proved exceedingly popular, and when Emily and Jamie laughed at her, she would smile back with glee.

Unexpected

It wasn't until the second week in May that Ellen finally heard that a decision had been reached by the looked-after children's team. Ellen had received a text from Graham at around 9 a.m. telling her that he would call her later that day to explain what would happen next. Ellen arrived early for contact that day, her face clouded with anxiety as she told me about Graham's message. 'I know what he's going to say,' she stated with near certainty. 'I don't think I'll even bother answering his call. Nothing ever goes right for me.' But her eyes were filled with hope.

For the next few hours, while I couldn't stop chatting, Ellen was mostly silent. Sitting on the floor with Hope propped up against her stomach, she ran her fingers over and over her hair, pulling it up into a tight bun and letting it unravel before bundling it up again. When Ellen's mobile rang just after 4 p.m., her face drained of colour. My legs went weak. She threw me a desperate look and stood, holding onto my hand tightly as she lifted the phone to her ear.

Two days later, when Hope was twelve weeks old, Ellen came to take her baby home. Their temporary separation was about to dissolve, and for me the moment was special, electric almost, but bittersweet as well; Hope held a special place in my heart, and over the weeks I had grown fond of Ellen as well, enjoying the unlikely companionship of our afternoons.

The sky was a clear blue, and warm air drifted into the hall as I opened the door with Hope balanced on my hip, her small suitcase, packed the evening before, standing on its side nearby. Ellen beamed when she saw us, reaching out and taking Hope, who kicked excitedly at the sight of her mum. Her hair was up, she had small silver studs in her ears and her eyes were alive with anticipation. I offered her a cup of tea but there were so many butterflies swirling in my stomach that I half hoped she would refuse. 'I'll get going, I think, Rosie,' she said, car keys jangling in her hand. 'I'm excited to show Hope her new room.'

I smiled. For most people, taking their own baby home was such an ordinary event – a happy one, but something that was taken for granted. It was easy to forget that, for some, life wasn't always as kind. 'Oh, yes, you must be. There's a bottle made up for her and the rest are sterilised. I've put a few cartons of ready-made SMA in there as well,' I said, handing Hope's nappy bag to her. 'Just so you get a chance to settle before having to think about chores.' Ellen caught the look on my face and, feeling exposed, I switched to my briskly efficient mode, patting Hope's back and planting a brief kiss on her forehead. 'Right, I'll help you to the car with her things.'

Ellen didn't move. 'Rosie?' she said, and there was something about her tone that stirred a fresh wave of emotion in me. A lump rose in my throat and I coughed. 'She'd probably be in someone else's arms now if it weren't for you,' she said, her voice quivering. Reaching out, she squeezed my hand. 'I'll never forget what you've done for us.'

More than a little choked, I pressed my lips together in a shaky smile. 'I'm so happy to help,' I managed to say before pulling them both into a hug. Foster carers are sometimes able to bridge the chasm that separates social workers from birth parents, and I've known many who have kept a relationship of sorts with a child's family, some maintaining friendships years after a placement has ended. As Ellen started the engine and headed towards her new life, I hoped that if she or Hope ever needed help in the future, she wouldn't hesitate to return. For my part, I would always be there for both of them.

Epilogue

I heard from Ellen often in the months following Hope's departure, mainly by way of panicked phone calls late in the evening. 'Her poop's gone bright yellow!' she'd shrieked without preamble the day after she took Hope home. 'That can't be right, surely!'

Later that week she discovered a lump at the back of Hope's neck which, after careful consultation on Google, she diagnosed as a tumour – it turned out to be one of her vertebrae. The next day she rang in a flap because she couldn't hear Hope breathing. 'Her chest's moving up and down, but not as much as usual.'

'Noisy breathing,' I said, trying to keep the amusement out of my tone, 'not so noisy breathing; it's all good.'

'I'm not one of those highly strung mothers who fly into a panic about everything, Rosie,' she'd said defensively.

I stayed silent. She started to see the funny side. 'Oh, what kind of madness is this?' she'd groaned, laughing in spite of herself.

Two weeks later, though, Ellen rang with some amazing news – Mark, Hope's biological father, had returned home. My guess was that her love for Hope had perhaps helped her to see that she was more than a product of her past, allowing her to move on and accept that she deserved to be happy.

I'm still fortunate enough to see the couple regularly, and it's a thrill to see Hope, now a happy and bright girl of nine, thriving in the warmth of Mark and Ellen's unconditional love.

Introduction by Rosie Lewis

I can remember the first time I read one of Casey Watson's fostering memoirs. It was at the end of one of *those* days early on in a placement, when the newly arrived children were bewildered and angry and particularly inventive when it came to finding ways to challenge me, and I was beginning to question my own ability to help them.

Reading Casey's book was like being invited into her home. Shining out from the pages, over and above her strength, kindness and determination to help the children in her care, was a gentle humour and sense of fun that seemed to carry her through the most difficult fostering days. What I found particularly inspiring was her candidness and her ability to admit that were times when she felt vulnerable, when she questioned herself and when she wasn't always sure of the way ahead. It was then that, like me, she was able to draw on the love and support of her family; her husband, Mike and her birth children.

Angels in Our Hearts

It is testament to Casey's skill as a writer that I feel as if I know the Watson family as well as I know my next-door neighbours, and so I am thrilled to be able to introduce these brief insights into their lives.

I'd like to dedicate this book to all my fellow foster carers, wherever you may be. I've never known a time when the service has been quite as stretched as it is today, not just in terms of the numbers of children needing care, but in the complexity and breadth of their problems. And I'm sure I'm not alone in feeling overwhelmed sometimes. Yet on we all go, because we know we can each make a difference. To quote the Dalai Lama, 'If you think you're too small to make a difference, try sleeping with a mosquito.' Hats off (if not mosquito nets) to you all.

Casey

CASEY WATSON

SUNDAY TIMES BESTSELLING AUTHOR

Just a Boy

An inspiring and heartwarming
short story

Just a Boy

Kindness is a language which the deaf
can hear and the blind can see.
Mark Twain

Dropping my shopping in the hall, car keys hanging from my mouth, I ran through the house to get to the phone before it cut off.

'Hello,' I spluttered, trying to catch my breath.

'Casey, hi there,' said a familiar voice. It was John Fulshaw, my fostering-agency link worker. 'You sound puffed,' he observed. 'Are you okay to talk?'

'To you?' I replied, laughing. 'Anytime. Do you bring me good tidings?' I felt a ripple of excitement about why he might be phoning. Mike and I were between placements at the moment, a state of affairs I became bored with very easily. Perhaps John had a new child for us. Now that would really make my Wednesday. 'Well?' I finished.

'Yes,' he said. 'I do.'

I was just about to ask him for chapter and verse when he continued. 'But only of a temporary nature. It's a four-teen-year-old boy who lives with his elderly grandparents and needs a place to stay just for a couple of days.'

He went on to explain that this boy, who was called Cameron, wouldn't be one of our usual kind of children, who mainly came from terrible backgrounds or were already in the care system. This was different. It was a lad who lived in perfectly agreeable family circumstances and who needed a place to go only because his grandmother had been taken ill and hospitalised. Apparently, Granddad, who was disabled, wouldn't be able to manage on his own, which was why a place needed to be found right away. He also needed to be able to spend time with his sick wife, John finished, and obviously couldn't be in two places at once.

'And our lad's a bit too much of a handful to be home alone then, is he?' I chortled. I knew what fourteen-year-old boys could be like.

'Not at all,' John corrected me. 'Quite the opposite – he'll be no trouble at all. There's just one thing you need to know, really. He's blind.'

For the first time in my life, I think, I was completely lost for words. I tried to recall if I'd ever even met anyone who was blind before, and couldn't, and then, of course, my brain starting whirring. What would it be like, having a blind child living with us? Would it be difficult? Would we need to move the furniture?

'Casey?' John prompted, obviously mistaking my logistical musings for reluctance. 'Don't feel obliged to say yes to this. We can ask someone else, I just thought you might be interested. I know you're itching to get another child in and I thought this might make an interesting stop-gap for you both. He's a lovely lad – really funny and doesn't let his disability faze him. Do you want some time to talk it over with Mike?'

'God, no,' I reassured him. 'Mike will be absolutely fine with it. I don't need to ask him because I know he'll say yes.'

'Well, if you're sure ...' John said. 'It would only be from tomorrow to Saturday morning. There's a family member travelling up to take over then, I believe, and –'

'*Sure* I'm sure,' I told him. So that was that.

As I expected, Mike wasn't fazed in the least. By the time he'd got home from work that afternoon, I'd already been busy on the internet, fact-finding. And it had been really useful. Taking inspiration from the website of a school for the blind, with their sensory rooms, musical instruments, interactive and soft play areas, I already had lots of ideas.

Mike seemed to find all this amusing. 'Soft play areas?' he asked. 'You said the lad was fourteen, didn't you? Not four! And if he's been blind from birth [something else I'd managed to clarify] I expect he's capable of a lot more than you think. Still,' he mused, looking around him, 'it does make you think, doesn't it? He's obviously familiar with his own surroundings but I reckon it will still be pretty challenging to navigate himself around here.' He closed his eyelids. 'And it'll certainly be an eye-opener for us, eh?'

Angels in Our Hearts

Mike's lame jokes aside, I felt quite excited about the following morning, and also a bit more prepared, having spent half the evening doing more research and finding out that, contrary to what I'd always thought, many blind people could see at least some things; could often distinguish daylight from night-time, and see blurry outlines of objects and people. So my idea of perpetual darkness wasn't correct at all. And I was about to learn more. I couldn't wait.

It seemed as if the weather was on my wavelength as well. Thursday morning dawned to match my mood – sunny and expectant. It seemed the British climate had, for a change, decided to be kind. It was mid August and for almost the first time that month, it seemed to be in accord with everyone's seasonal expectations.

'Uh-oh,' said my grown-up son Kieron as he came down to the kitchen. 'Do I smell bleach? Honestly, Mother, at *this* time?' He did. I was on my hands and knees, giving the floor a last once over. We had a dog – Bob – and I was conscious that with a visitor coming to stay, mucky paw marks were a no-no, even if the visitor couldn't see them.

Kieron stepped over me to get to the cereal cupboard. He had a busy day planned, going off with a mate of his to pick an amp up from some far-flung location; Kieron was in college, but had being earning a few quid over the summer DJing and was doing a disco at the local youth club on Friday night.

'You do,' I said, 'and talking of smells, can you do me a

favour? Can you nip out to the garden before you go and pick what you can find for me, flowers-wise?'

It would be nice, I thought, bearing in mind what I'd read about sensory-impaired people relying more on their other senses, to have the place smelling nice for Cameron's arrival.

Kieron duly did, and, in fact, still hadn't left when the car containing Cameron pulled up outside. Though not with John – there was no need for John to be involved in this handover. There'd be no reams of paperwork, no ominous-looking manila files to be gone through; just a quick chat with Cameron's social worker, Jeremy.

I went to the front door and opened it ready, taking stock as the two of them approached. It felt a little weird watching someone so intently when they couldn't see you, but my eyes were drawn to him as if by a magnet. He was a tall lad – he looked more like sixteen or seventeen than fourteen – and good-looking, too, with a shock of conker-coloured hair. I noticed straight away that he walked without the aid of his social worker and instead had a white cane that snapped into life when he shook it, and sort of hovered, just above ground level, swinging left and right in front of him, as he deftly made his way to our door.

I didn't know what he could see of me, but Cameron had a huge smile on his face, and appeared to be looking just above my head. This was no surprise really, given the difference in our height. I'm four foot eleven, and this kid had to be six feet tall. I was just about to say hello when I almost jumped out of my skin. Out of nowhere, this robotic-sounding voice had suddenly spoken. 'Good morning,' it said. 'It is 10.00 a.m.'

Cameron laughed and turned his head. 'That's a fiver you owe me, Jezza,' he said to his social worker. 'Told you we wouldn't be late, didn't I?'

Jeremy seemed amused by my startled expression, 'Talking watch,' he said by way of explanation. 'We had a bit of a bet on the way over, because I was getting in a bit of a fluster about being late, and Cameron – he's a bit of a whizz with numbers, aren't you, Cameron? – had a wager with me. And it looks like he won.' He grinned at his charge. 'But it was for a cream cake, not a fiver. Bit of a chancer, this one,' he chuckled.

I shook Jeremy's hand. 'Come on in,' I said.

'And mind the step!' Kieron added. He and Bob were now just behind me, having obviously come to say hello.

'Oh, that's okay,' Cameron shot back, deftly crossing the threshold unaided. 'My stick has built-in radar so I knew about that step a few inches before I touched it.'

Kieron and I looked at each other and I was just about to say something dumb when Cameron added, 'That was a joke, by the way.'

It set the tone perfectly, and it was with jovial spirits that we had our mini-meeting. It seemed Cameron did have some basic vision – dark and light, some fuzzy shapes and muted colours – and, between them, he and Jeremy explained the practical things about safety, as well as what Cameron liked to eat and 'watch' on TV. This surprised me. It never occurred to me that a blind person might enjoy television, but apparently he did, very much so. In fact, it turned out he was a whizz with a TV remote, and showed me something I'd never realised; that there was a reason for the little knobble on the number five button – it was the point visually impaired people could navigate from. There was even such a thing as 'audio description', which I'd also never heard of – some programmes had a narrator describing the scenes as they occurred to make it easier to picture as you listened to the programme. Amazing! I thought.

Twenty minutes later, Jeremy had to set off, having scribbled down his mobile number for emergencies, handed me a slim file of information, and assured me he would be back on Saturday afternoon to pick Cameron up. We said our goodbyes and then I went back into the dining room where we had left Cameron, to find him engaged in conversation with Kieron.

'Ah, Mum,' Kieron said. 'There are rules to having Cameron here, so listen up.'

I blinked at him. My son is lovely, but his Asperger's can make him rather inclined to rules and regulations, and I had visions of him interrogating the poor boy relentlessly.

'Don't you have to be somewhere?' I asked him.

But Kieron shook his head. 'Not till lunchtime now,' he said, waving his mobile phone at me. 'Joe's gotta do some stuff first. Plus I have to walk Bob for you …'

'For me?' I asked drily. Bob was very much Kieron's dog, he being the one who'd just turned up with him, fresh from the dogs' home, after all. 'Anyway,' he went on, 'we've just been chatting and Cam's been telling me some of the stuff you need to know. And first up is that if you leave a room, you always have to say so. Just so he knows, and doesn't jump out of his skin when you come back.'

'Ri-ight,' I said, noting Cameron's approving nod. 'And the next one?'

'Doors,' said Kieron. 'That's right, isn't it?'

Cameron nodded again. 'Yup. It's important that they're always left closed or fully open. Otherwise I have a tendency to bang into them.'

'Ouch,' I said, glancing at the door into the hall, which – as ever – was neither one nor the other. I went and pulled it fully open.

'Tell you what,' I said. 'Kieron, since you're the official keeper of the rules, why don't you give Cameron the guided tour while I make us all some drinks, yes? And – erm – I'm leaving the room now, Cameron, okay?'

Both boys immediately burst out laughing. Which made me relax. This was going to be fine.

As I'd suggested, Kieron gave Cameron the full tour of the house, and as I watched them go upstairs I noticed how methodical Cameron was about it, seeming to calculate steps and distances between things. When they returned I also noticed that he'd come down without his cane.

'Do you want me to nip back up and fetch it down for you?' I asked, after pointing it out.

'No, it's fine, Casey,' he assured me. 'I only need it once for round the house, then I can trail to navigate.'

'Tail?' I asked. 'That sounds like something the FBI might do.'

Both Kieron and Cameron laughed then. Again. 'He said "trail", Mum, not "tail",' Kieron corrected me.

Cameron grinned. 'I'll show you,' he said, walking into the front room and crossing it without hesitation, simply using the back of his hand against the wall, slightly in front of him. Again, I could see he was making constant calculations, having presumably already made a mental map. 'See?' he said. 'Simple! No cane required.'

Kieron looked at his phone again, this time to check the time. 'And I need to crack on,' he said. 'Bob – walkies!'

Bob duly left his basket in the kitchen and trotted in, tail wagging.

'Have you ever had a guide dog?' I asked Cameron, as Kieron went to fetch Bob's lead.

'No,' he said. 'I'd love a dog, but it would be too much for my grandparents.'

'Want to come with me to walk Bob, then?' Kieron asked, coming back in.

'Erm, I'm not sure that's ...' I began.

'No, it's fine,' Cameron said. 'I'd really like that. If it's all right with you, Casey,' he said politely.

Still I hesitated. I was *in loco parentis*, after all. Was he safe outside without me? Was he normally allowed out on his own? But Kieron – nineteen, and a responsible adult – pulled a face at me.

'Mum, we'll only be walking to the end of the road and back!' he pointed out. 'What's gonna happen?'

So I went and fetched the cane after all.

* * *

The first afternoon and evening went like a dream. Used to dealing with the sort of challenging kids that tested you every step of the way, I enjoyed every moment of getting to know Cameron, and 'looking after him' seemed a contradiction in terms.

With the whole 'sensory experiences' thing very much in mind, I took him to a local park once Kieron had gone, one that had a big and popular petting zoo. And it was a good choice; Cameron loved petting the goats and alpacas and everywhere we went people were just so nice to him. We then went for ice creams and visited the zoo shop, where I helped him pick out a postcard for his grandmother.

'I always get her postcards from wherever I've been,' he said. She's not very mobile any more but loves to be able to see what I've been up to. She has quite a collection these days!'

Talking further, it transpired that Cameron got about quite a bit. Though he lived happily at home with his grandparents, his single mum having died in an accident when he was very little, they had worked hard to provide him with a normal active childhood, supported by his school and a variety of organisations which could introduce him to the wider world. For all his lack of street-awareness – which was a big change from the kids I usually fostered – he had a wise and mature head on his young shoulders.

And I was anxious to make sure he had a fun time while he was with us. So when another glance at his file told me the things he most liked doing, I was determined that we'd do one of them, too.

'Bowling?' Mike said, as he was putting on his jacket for work the following morning, and I was giving him the run-down on what I'd planned. I'd already told him I thought we should take Cameron out somewhere together before he left us, and that he was to try his very best to get away from work early.

'Yes, bowling,' I repeated. 'He's rather good at it apparently.'

'But how can he bowl a bowling ball? It just sounds so dangerous!'

'Well, you'll soon find out, won't you?' I said to him, laughing. 'Now remember. Home by four, and no excuses!'

He shook his head as he headed out of the door. 'Bowling?' I heard him muttering to himself. '*Bowling*?'

Truth was that I had no idea how he did it either. I only knew that it was a good plan. Cameron was thrilled to hear what we'd be doing and promised me that he was super-good at it and would embarrass us with his skill for sure. I had no doubt he would, at least as far as I was concerned, because I was rubbish. In fact, I had never understood the thrill of picking up a heavy ball, inserting your fingers into holes where someone else's grubby mitts had been, and then chucking it at a load of pins. Still, it would be fun for Cameron and that was what it was all about. Taking his mind off his sick gran for a bit.

And of course, Cameron had been telling the truth. Eschewing the frame the visually impaired would normally use, he really could seem to 'feel' his way to a strike, and duly kicked our butts. Particularly mine, and I was left astounded at how I – equipped with full vision – could be so roundly thrashed by a boy with hardly any. And worse than that, everyone knew it, the bowling alley having thoughtfully employed a system that rang out a loud noise every time a ball hit the gutter, which almost all of mine did.

But perhaps I was becoming too used to being amazed by Cameron's abilities, because what happened straight afterwards I didn't see coming.

We were just gathering our stuff, ready to go and grab some dinner, when my attention was diverted by Cameron leaving our booth with his coke can. My gaze followed him, but only in a vague 'Where's he off to?' way when, to my horror, I then saw him casually lob the can at the man sitting reading a newspaper just behind the next booth. Worse than that, even, was that the can wasn't quite empty, and I watched with dismay as a stream of coke shot from the can and fell like sticky rain all down the man's shirt.

'Oi!' he said, rising and brushing down his shirt simultaneously. 'Oi! What the hell d'you think you're doing?'

By this time, Cameron had already turned around and was walking back to us, seemingly oblivious to what he had just done. But no longer. The man's voice positively boomed across the lane.

I watched Cameron's face fall. 'Oh, no!' he said, obviously realising what must have happened. 'Oh, I'm so sorry,' he added, turning back towards the man. 'I had no idea. I thought you were the bin!'

The man threw down the newspaper he had in his other hand and marched up to Cameron, his face reddening in anger. He grabbed Cameron's arm. 'Oh, so you're a joker as well, are you, you little git?'

Mike was suddenly there then, a reassuring presence. At six foot three, and given the expression on the man's face, a *very* reassuring presence. Because he really looked like he was ready to punch Cameron.

'Hey there,' Mike said evenly. 'Calm down, mate, okay? Whatever happened, it was obviously an accident.'

'Accident?' the man said. 'This moron just threw a coke can at me!'

'It was an accident!' Cameron added quickly. His head was bobbing about and I could see he wasn't sure where to rest his gaze now, as Mike and the man must be blurring together. 'I'm really sorry. But I really did think you were the bin, honest. The way you were sitting, and ...'

'The way I was *sitting*?' the man blustered. 'Oh, that's rich, that is, you little sh–'

'Hey,' said Mike again, positioning himself between both of them. 'Calm *down*, will you, mate? He's *blind*. Can't you *see* that?'

The man was so worked up that it took a couple of seconds for him to register, but when the penny dropped it really did drop. I finally allowed myself to unclench my hands and breathe out.

'Oh,' the man muttered, the fight slowly draining out of him, as he realised his mistake. But not completely. He still had a look of aggression about him. And he clearly had a tongue to match, too. 'Well, you should keep him indoors, then,' he barked, 'if he can't bloody see! Bloody menace! You should ****ing keep him in!' And with that, he stomped back to his soggy paper, while I stood there, gobsmacked that he could be so cruel.

Cameron was mortified. 'I need to go and apologise again,' he said to Mike as we ushered him away. 'Was he very wet? I should offer to pay for his shirt to be cleaned, at the very least.'

My heart went out to him. His lower lip was wobbling and I could see he was really shaken. As was I. That sort of aggression might be exciting on the telly, but in the real world it was very, very frightening.

'Love, it was an accident,' I tried to reassure hm. 'And you have already apologised. Come on, let's get out of here,' I said. 'Let's go and get some tea.'

He didn't seem convinced. 'I thought he was the bin, I really did. It was the way he was sitting … I should really …' He tailed off then and I could see he was struggling not to cry. I was just glad he couldn't see what Mike and I could: the number of curious pairs of eyes that were on us. Some pitying, some just staring, as if Cameron was a freak show.

I couldn't wait to get out of there and, as we left, I glanced back towards the man. It was so obvious now how easy a mistake it had been to make. His shirt was almost the same red as the bowling booths themselves, and with the newspaper open in front of him … well, I could easily see how it might have happened. 'Please don't be upset,' I said, squeezing Cameron's arm. 'He's just a very rude man, so –'

'So he's lost any right to an apology, in my book,' Mike finished. His expression was set and grim. 'What a …'

He just about managed to stop himself saying what he was thinking. Instead he mouthed it. And I heard it loud and clear.

The incident at the bowling alley coloured the rest of the evening, with Cameron no longer the sunny lad who'd arrived the day before. He was quiet, and though we kept telling him to forget all about it, I could tell he was racked with mortification about what he'd done. He spoke to his granddad before bed, and while I was in the kitchen making drinks for us all, I could hear him telling him what a complete dork he'd been.

'We shouldn't have taken him,' I said to Mike once we were tucked up under the duvet.

'What?' he said. 'Casey, that's just mad, that is, honestly. Whyever not? He obviously goes all the time.' He grinned ruefully, recalling having been so roundly beaten. 'So why on earth *wouldn't* we have taken him?'

'I know,' I said. 'But I should have thought it through more. It's not the bowling alley he's used to going to, is it? So he didn't know his way around. If he had it wouldn't have happened.'

'Nothing *happened*,' Mike persisted. 'That man was just

a joke – anyone could see that. The whole thing was just a storm in a teacup.'

'Trickle in a coke can,' I corrected. But for all my jesting, I still felt guilty for having taken him, as the things that horrible man had said ran round and round my head.

But I was to come down the following morning to an even greater shock. Waking early, after a broken night, to see that another glorious day had dawned, I was determined that Cameron should leave us on a high note rather than a low one. So, leaving everyone to enjoy lie-ins, I tiptoed across the landing with the idea of cooking up a huge full English breakfast, which I'd serve in the garden, on the patio table.

Seeing Cameron's bedroom door open, though, and his bed made and empty, I assumed he must have beaten me to it – very atypical for a fourteen-year-old boy, but then, Cameron wasn't a very typical fourteen-year-old boy, was he? Perhaps he was busy 'watching' some TV. But when I got downstairs to find no sign of him there either, I was flummoxed. Where could he be?

I ran back upstairs to double-check he wasn't in the bathroom, even though I knew he wasn't – I'd only passed it seconds earlier.

'Mike,' I hissed, shaking him awake. 'Cameron's disappeared! I can't find him anywhere. Oh, God, do you think he's run away?'

Mike rubbed his eyes and sat up. 'Run away?' He looked amused. 'Have you been at the gin, love? Why on earth would he do that? Don't be silly.'

'Honest, Mike. He is nowhere to be found. And the back door is on the latch, too. So where is he? Come on, get dressed. We have to go out and try and find him!'

Mike duly pulled on trackie bottoms and trainers and followed me out into the street, blinking in the sunshine like an oversized frightened rabbit. We went all round the block and down several other streets, but he was nowhere to be found, and a familiar gnawing in my gut started up. We'd had runaways before – it was one of the grimmest 'perks' of doing fostering – but to lose a placid fourteen-year-old, only in our care for two days, felt like the biggest failure imaginable. I was also fearful about him heading out alone, possibly into traffic. Was he really as independent as he seemed? And why had he gone? Had he just had enough? Was he on some mission? Had he decided to try and make it to the hospital?

'None of the above,' Mike assured me, trying to quell my rising panic. 'He's a well-brought-up boy and he just wouldn't *do* something like that.'

'But what do *we* do?' I asked him anxiously.

'We go back home and make a plan.'

Mike was right, of course. It was completely out of character for Cameron to run away. But even so – even if he'd just gone on a wander – we still faced the grim task of calling Jeremy and telling him our 'charge' was no longer under our charge. And by the time we got back, called his number and left a voice message, I was becoming more and more agitated. He hadn't taken his holdall, but he had taken his stick. Oh, God, I thought, where had he gone?

It was still early – not far past eight yet – so it wasn't surprising that it was a while before our anxious reveries were interrupted by the sudden sound of ringing, which made us jump. But it wasn't the phone, it was the doorbell, which we both rushed to get to, to be rewarded by a reassuring bulky shadow beyond the glass.

Mike opened the door. 'Cameron!' he exclaimed. 'Where've you been, lad?'

I took in the scene: Cameron, looking sheepish, and an elderly gentleman I vaguely recognised, who introduced himself as Mr Parsons, and who, though looking only slightly less bemused than we were, had a definite twinkle in his eye.

'This one belong to you?' he asked, grinning.

'Yes,' I said. 'Yes, he does. Cameron, what *happened*?'

Cameron's face was turning the same colour as next door's roses. 'I'm so sorry,' he said, frowning. 'I feel such an idiot.'

'Found him a couple of streets away,' Mr Parsons said, 'on my way back from getting my paper. So I took him indoors, gave him a drink – it's a hot old morning to be traipsing the streets, eh? And it took a little time to fathom out where he belonged, but between us we got there, didn't we, son?'

'I'm sorry …' Cameron began again.

Mr Parsons chortled. 'Sorry? Not a bit of it! Most entertaining Saturday morning I've had in a long time, believe me. And a pleasure to meet you, young man!'

* * *

Waving Mr Parsons off with our undying gratitude, we bundled Cameron back indoors for a debrief.

'Where were you off to?' I wanted to know, trying not to sound like I was chastising him. I was conscious that he'd been with us less than forty-eight hours and seemed to be apologising right, left, and centre.

But it turned out he hadn't been running away. In fact, the idea brought a smile to his lips. 'Casey, I think I'm the last person on earth who should try running away from anywhere, don't you?'

All he'd wanted to do was post a letter. Well, more correctly, a postcard, to his gran. It was the one from the petting zoo which, unbeknown to either Mike or me, he'd had Kieron write and address for him the previous evening, just before going off to do his DJing.

'I know I didn't *need* to,' he said. 'I could just as easily have given it to her when I go and see her next week. But Granddad had told me she was feeling low last night, and I was awake and the sun was shining and since I'd passed the letter box with Kieron on Thursday, I knew where it was … And I just thought it would be nice for her to get it brought round in the post. But, somehow – I don't know *how* –'

'You got yourself well and truly lost,' Mike said, chuckling.

Cameron nodded. 'Exactly. I should have only been gone two minutes. Except –' he glanced towards his stick, which was resting beside his leg. 'Flipping radar,' he said. 'Rubbish, it is. Rubbish.'

* * *

So in the end, Cameron *did* leave us on a high note, because we all laughed so hard it even roused Kieron from his slumbers, and we had our full English in the garden just as planned. And I think we all learned something good from our encounter. Cameron that his navigation wasn't quite as infallible as he thought; that in Mr Parsons we have a very nice neighbour; and well, in my case, that I do have a tendency to panic, because I do – as Kieron's pointed out time and again over the years – take things so much to heart where people being mean to kids is concerned. Cameron had been quiet because he'd been thinking about his gran, not because of what the ignorant man had said at the bowing alley. He told us he'd be mad to – that he wasn't worth the head-space. 'Water off a duck's back,' he quipped, when he left us.

'Or coke down a shirt front!' Mike corrected, which meant I learned something else: my husband's jokes really don't get any better.

We got a lovely thank-you card from Cameron a couple of weeks after he left us, and I shall treasure it always. Inside it was a quote from that most famous of blind people, Helen Keller, and a lovely one for anyone to bear in mind: *The only thing worse than being blind is having sight but no vision.*

A lesson for us all. And as Mike predicted, an eye-opening two days.

CASEY WATSON

SUNDAY TIMES BESTSELLING AUTHOR

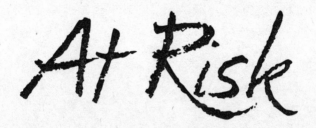

At Risk

An innocent boy.
A sinister secret.
Is there no one
to save him from
danger?

Chapter 1

Friday

It wasn't like me to have a headache. Headaches had a very specific place in my life. They came via school holidays, chocolate and/or an excess of grandchildren, none of which currently applied. Still, the thumping going on above my head – Tyler packing upstairs, in his usual Tyler fashion – was accompanied by a definite thumping in my head, so I reached into the medicine cabinet that I kept in the kitchen cupboard and popped two paracetamol from their foil sheet.

'Feeling sorry for yourself?' Mike asked as he joined me in the kitchen.

'No,' I replied tartly. 'I just have a headache. Must be the change in the season or something.'

He stopped pouring coffee and gave me a hug. 'Aww – worried about being all on your lonesome, love? Is that it? But you'll find something to occupy yourself,' he pointed out, reasonably. 'So stop looking so miserable. It's only just over a week. Besides, Kieron and Lauren will no doubt be around with Dee Dee, so –'

'I am *not* feeling sorry for myself,' I said again, firmly. Though, actually, truth be known, I sort of was.

'Yes you are. But it's your own fault. You could have come with us.'

I made a 'tsk' sound, somewhat irritably, because that was true as well. Except, *really*? Me on a school skiing trip? In the *cold*?

There was no getting away from it, of course. That Mike was right – there *had* been nothing stopping me. It was the last week of the spring term, Easter just on the horizon, and, as Tyler, our permanent foster child, was going on the trip, it wasn't as if I had anyone to stay home *for*. And with my daughter-in-law Lauren, David and their kids already en route to Cornwall as we spoke – for ten days, no less – that was doubly true. And it wasn't as if I didn't like snow. I loved snow. Just in the right place and time, that was all. At Christmas, and mostly on the outside.

No, it was the time of year when my thoughts turned to beaches and sunshine, and though Tyler assured me his teacher had promised plenty of the latter, the thought of donning ski gear and hefty snow boots, and generally slipping and sliding around the place, held about as much appeal for me as bungee jumping – i.e. none at all.

I still couldn't quite believe Mike had been so keen on it. That he'd actually *agreed* to go along to be a helper. After all, who could he actually help? He'd skied precisely once in his life. When he was seven. Perhaps that was why my head hurt – because of the sheer incredulity of it all.

I swallowed my tablets with the glass of orange juice Mike had thoughtfully poured for me, just as the upstairs thumps and bangs resolved themselves into a resounding thud out in the hall.

'Don't worry!' Tyler shouted down the stairs, getting in before I could berate him. 'That was just my rucksack! I threw it down so I can carry my other stuff,' he added helpfully.

I poked my head out into the hall, seeing the rucksack and feeling a little pang of something I didn't quite like. Tyler had never been away for eight whole days before. And never so far away. 'Not like you couldn't have made two trips!' I shouted back.

'Well, that's going to do your head a *lot* of good,' Mike observed, grinning.

For all that I was a bit 'fomo' – that was the term Tyler had used, wasn't it? – my 'fear of missing out', which had turned out to be more acute than I'd expected, still wasn't a match for the excitement I felt on Tyler's behalf. He'd been on about the school ski trip since it had first been mooted the previous summer, and though we'd provided the money for most of it as part of his Christmas present, he had been saving hard and earning extra pocket money for it ever since. He couldn't have been more excited if he'd tried, bless him. And when one of the parent-helpers had to pull out, having broken their ankle (which felt

ironic), he'd been beyond thrilled when Mike said he'd –
ahem – 'step in' instead.

Whereas I'd been beyond open-mouthed in shock at
Mike not so much voluntarily offering to go skiing but
going away for a week with a coachload of over-excited
teenagers. But apparently it was all go-go-go. He had a
week's leave to use up before Easter, and though the
30-hour coach trip held a measure of concern for him he
was looking forward to the trip itself almost as much as
Tyler. 'Like riding a bike, it is, you'll see' – he'd said that a
dozen times, if not more. Trouble was, I wouldn't. I'd have
to wait for the videos.

I gave myself a mental shake and started making breakfast for them both. Least I could do. Goodness only knew
when they'd get their next proper meal. So bacon and eggs
as a special treat, I thought. And I decided as I stood and
watched the bacon begin sizzling that it was time to pull on
my big-girl pants and stop being a baby.

Well, only up to a point. Since I was charged with taking
the two of them down to the school gates at the allotted
time of ten, there was no way I was going to turn straight
around and drive home again.

'Oh, gawd, you're not going hang around and show me
up, are you?' Tyler groaned as he added his rucksack to the
growing pile by the side of the coach and, while Mike went
off to bond with all the accompanying teachers, submitted
to a kiss and a hug.

'You really need me to even answer that?' I said. 'Now go
on, get on the coach before all the window seats have gone,

or you won't be able to see me running down the road alongside with tears streaming down my face, will you?'

Tyler groaned again and made a face at his friend Denver, who'd just arrived. 'Honest,' he told him. 'My mum is just *the* most embarrassing parent, *ever*.'

Tyler had been with us long enough now that it often occurred to me that him calling me 'mum' to his friends should feel normal. It didn't. I still got a lump in my throat every time. And it took a huge effort of will, once the coach was ready to leave, not to do exactly what I'd threatened. As it was, after issuing threats about what I'd do to them if they didn't phone me every single night, I let them go with just a stoic and queenly wave.

Then headed home, thinking what a weird week it would be. Quiet-weird. Not weird-weird. Well, in theory …

By half past eleven I was back in the zone at home – the radio blaring, the doors wide open and my cleaning materials spread out on the kitchen worktops, my headache spirited away on the breeze. Spring was here, the sun was shining, and I had decided to stop moping and instead make the most of my unexpected free time.

I was two hours in, singing as I wiped down the cooker, when my plans were wiped out at a stroke.

Or, rather at the ringing of my mobile. John Fulshaw. My fostering agency link worker. 'Hi, Casey,' he said chattily, 'can you talk?'

He sounded fine. Which was unusual. Normally, if I wasn't expecting him, his voice would sound urgent, because, normally, it meant an emergency. 'I can,' I said, peeling off a rubber glove with my teeth. 'What's up?'

'I was just phoning on the off chance,' he said. 'I wouldn't normally ask you, and I know you probably have lots of plans, but I was just wondering if you were free for a couple of days. We need someone to take an 11-year-old boy, as an emergency. We're really stuck. It seems like everyone's going away.'

'Not me,' I said, then explained about it only being Mike and Tyler. Which was important, because it meant I was at home by myself and that precluded me from taking certain children. There would be no point in John telling me all about this boy if he was the type that had historically attacked single female carers, or who had a background of abuse from a female.

But John was quick to reassure me that Adam – for that was the little boy's name – wasn't going to present challenges of that kind. Of any kind, apparently.

'Oh, no worries there, Casey,' John reassured me. 'It's a pretty straightforward one, this. Adam's only ever lived with his mum – no father ever in the picture – so he's used to being with just one carer anyway. He's not in the system at all, as it happens. This is simply a case of his mother being rushed into hospital for an emergency appendectomy, and he has no family to look after him. Simple as. In fact, he's at school as we speak, and as yet has no idea that he can't go home this afternoon, so you can see how we're fixed.'

'That's it?' I asked, because I had long, long experience of John's relationship with the words 'straightforward' and 'a couple of days'. Not his fault, obviously – sometimes the most straightforward-looking placements in the world turned out to be the most complicated once you scratched beneath the surface. And sobering too was the fact that you could be living a perfectly straightforward-seeming life, but with no family to provide support in the event of a crisis you really could have your life turned upside down.

'That's it,' John confirmed.

'Just till his mum is on the mend?' I asked, it occurring to me that it must be a pretty lonely life if you didn't even have a friend who could help you out at such a time. But then, all lives were different, and some very lonely.

'Just till she's able to be discharged,' John said. 'Couple of days or so. Probably just till the beginning of next week. And before you ask, no, there are no other problems.'

I could hear John chuckle. 'None that we are aware of, at least,' he added, 'and no, it's definitely not one of those calls where I promise it's only for the weekend when in reality I have nowhere else to place him on Monday. This really is a genuine emergency, and just for a few days, I can assure you.'

'Right then,' I said, as I pulled off the second glove with my free hand, 'I'll take him. I have nothing else to do this week – the whole tribe are away. Not just Mike and Tyler. So what's the plan?'

John explained that the school Adam attended was only a couple of miles away and that someone from social services would be going there at lunchtime. There, with the help of Adam's teacher, they would explain what had happened to his mother. I would meet them all at the school, we'd do the usual introductions, and then it was just a case of me bringing Adam home with me. It was as simple as that. We'd go to visit his mum in hospital as soon as she came out of surgery (she, of course, bless her, already knew the plan), and the moment she was fit enough, and home again, I would hand him back to her. A pretty everyday crisis placement all round.

And, at first sight, there was nothing about Adam to cause me to think he'd be anything other than straightforward. He was a sweet-looking lad, and tiny as well – seeming a good couple of years younger than his 11 years. The kind of lad you couldn't quite imagine going into high school in a few months, for sure. He was also pale and, while it might partly have been to do with shock, it was a more sallow kind of pale; as though he hadn't had enough sunlight in a very long time. He looked nervously at me through glasses that were too big for him and kept slipping off his nose, and he also seemed markedly underweight.

On the flip side, however, his school uniform was impeccable. I wondered if he must have a fresh one for every day, because it was remarkably clean and neat-looking for the last day of the school week. His hair, which was thick and the colour of milk chocolate, was clean, shiny and well cut as well. This made me happy. Little things, perhaps, but they added up to a big mental tick; his mum clearly took good care of him.

I introduced myself and sat beside him on the small chair in the head's office. 'I'm so sorry about your mum, sweetie,' I told him, 'but I will phone the hospital as soon as we get to mine, and arrange for us to go and visit her. Is that okay?'

I watched Adam assess me, in much the same way as I'd assessed him. Then he nodded, offering a polite smile, which was impressive under the circumstances. 'Thank you, miss,' he said quietly.

'It's Casey,' I corrected. 'And this is yours, I take it?' I gestured towards the small blue cabin-bag-sized case, which I presumed the social worker had obtained, and filled, in consultation with mum.

Adam nodded. As did the head, Mr Morris. 'Indeed it is,' he said briskly. 'Now, Adam, I wonder if you'd like to take yourself and your things outside for a moment, yes? Just while I deal with the paperwork with Mrs Watson.'

Adam meekly filed out, flanked by both his teacher and the social worker – *his* social worker for the short duration of his time in the system. Though nothing in his demeanour betrayed it, I didn't doubt he was in a state of some distress.

'I just thought you might have a few questions,' Mr Morris said. 'Bit of background and so on. Didn't want to talk over the lad, obviously.'

I thanked him. 'So is there anything to tell? Anything you think I should know?'

'Actually, no, not a lot,' Mr Morris said. 'He's a quiet lad, is Adam. Doesn't have too many friends, keeps himself to himself. But good as gold when he's here.'

I picked up on that. Adam didn't quite seem to fit the mould of a persistent truant. 'When he's here?'

'Always been a bit of a sickly child,' Mr Morris explained. 'Has a lot of time off ill with this and that. You know how it goes. Though according to his mother, he's undergoing some investigations or other ...'

'What kind?' I asked.

'To see what's wrong with him, essentially. Some sort of digestive problem has been mooted – he's apparently sick a lot. As in sick-sick. So, of course, if he has an episode she likes to keep him at home.'

I nodded. Adam's weight certainly seemed to bear that out. And some kids – well, they just weren't terribly robust. So this was apparently one such.

I smiled and thanked him. Nothing there to be concerned about, clearly. A straightforward lad and a straightforward placement – though, me being me, I couldn't resist doing what's a part of my very DNA – already thinking about fattening him up. Just a little. Just to put a bit of colour in his cheeks.

'All set, then?' I asked him as I joined him and the social worker back out in the school vestibule.

Adam nodded, and as I went to take the case handle from him I was surprised when he slipped his hand into mine instead. Reflexive mainly, I imagined – an adult extended a hand and a child of a certain age would often take it. But this was a lad of 11, which made it quite unusual. It also made me warm to him. He was prepared to put his trust in me, which touched me. 'So, almost Easter,' I remarked as we crossed the school car park. 'Which means it's like the law that I buy you some chocolate eggs this week, don't you think?'

It's a cliché to say a child's eyes light up, admittedly, but in Adam's case they really did seem to. Seemed I was going to have a pleasant week after all.

Chapter 2

Saturday

I woke early, because of birdsong rather than the tyranny of the alarm clock, and for a moment I forgot that I had a houseguest across the landing; I was too preoccupied with the unusual business of no Mike snoring beside me in the bed.

Then it hit me, and I wondered about the little lad I'd taken on. How had he slept? *Had* he slept, even? It must all seem so strange. We took in all sorts of children from all sorts of backgrounds and, usually, the urgent need for those children to be rescued – and more often than not, rehabilitated – was both the guiding light and the driving force. But Adam was different. He wanted nothing more than to be reunited with his loving mother, and when my phone call to the hospital the previous evening established that he couldn't (his mum wasn't apparently well enough to see him, being still so groggy from the anaesthetic) he was understandably anxious and upset.

At Risk

So I turned to my trusty games box for support, and, to my surprise, as we rummaged through the various board games and puzzles, Adam professed a great keenness to play chess – a game that mostly sat unloved and gathering dust, mostly down to my inability to play it with anything remotely approaching competence.

Which I quickly pointed out. 'Then I'll teach you, miss,' Adam told me, sounding altogether brighter as he carried the battered box to the dining room table.

'It's Casey,' I reminded him – for about the fifth time since we'd got home. 'And, believe me,' I added, in my Winston Churchill voice, 'many have tried, and few have succeeded.'

This pronouncement managed to elicit a giggle from Adam, which pleased me greatly, even if it did reinforce the feeling that Adam saw himself as having been billeted with a funny little mad lady for the duration.

Well, so be it, I thought, as I watched him place all the pieces. Bookish, I decided. Shy yet self-possessed. Not one for a great deal of socialising. And a boy, I decided, who would take any game he was playing very seriously.

I mentally smiled. He'd have no trouble beating me at this one. The intricacies of the game had always baffled me since back in childhood, and I had never really quite got the hang of it. I suspected I knew why, as well. A psychologist might correctly diagnose that I was mostly prevented from learning how to play such games by my inability to want to beat an opponent. Much as I loved the strategy of figuring out moves – and could even see how I could make counter-moves to avoid defeat – I simply couldn't find it in me to muster the required ruthlessness; it was so much my nature to allow the underdog to win, at all costs.

Happily, in this case, it was me who was the underdog and Adam proved deft in destroying me. Despite his many moments of explaining exactly *how* he was winning, he had me checkmated in no time at all. 'I know,' I said, after he'd beaten me a second time (and I reflected that this was unlike any fostering situation I'd ever known), 'how about I get my craft box out instead?'

Dressing-gowned-up now, and satisfied that Adam was sleeping soundly, I padded down to the kitchen and picked up the resultant work of art, which we'd left on the kitchen table to dry out. It stuck me anew that it was a bit of an odd choice.

Adam had decided to paint a picture of what I assumed was his mum, laid out in a hospital bed with various wires and tubes attached, and with some kind of machine at her side. He'd even attached a drip to her arm, complete with bag and stand.

It was actually rather good. There was no denying his talent. And in terms of technical details, it was spot on. But still an odd choice, given my suggestion that he paint something specifically to take *to* his mother – I'd assumed he'd do some flowers, or a landscape, or self-portrait, with the usual accompanying 'get well soon' message.

Still, I thought, as I put it down and went to fill the kettle, who was I to suggest what he should or shouldn't draw? Perhaps he had a future as a technical artist, or perhaps as a designer of some miraculous new scanner. He was certainly a bright enough boy.

Not to mention a hungry one. On that front he'd really surprised me, and while I had no idea what he most liked for breakfast, the evidence of the previous night's tea seemed to suggest that the answer was probably 'anything and everything'. He'd sat down to eat – tiny, underweight thing that he was – and proceeded to act like a small human vacuum cleaner, sucking up whatever appeared in front of him. Fish and chips, in this case, with lashings of curry sauce, along with several slices of bread and butter, then biscuits and milk, then some toast and a bar of chocolate while he painted his creation, then a drinking chocolate and yet another biscuit before bed. His family must have some seriously good genes, I remembered thinking, for him to have an appetite like that and still stay so thin. If that was his diet, then I wanted to be on it!

But, being Saturday, it was too early to think about breakfast anyway so, coffee made, I headed out into our sunny conservatory to give Mike and Tyler a quick call. According to the handout I'd been left with, which detailed their itinerary, they should by now have arrived in the resort. Plus they were an hour ahead, so I was keen to fill Mike in on my news before they headed off up the slopes.

'You've *what*?' Mike asked after I got through to his mobile and told him that I'd taken in a child only hours after he had left.

The anxiety in his voice was perfectly reasonable. The sorts of children we normally specialised in fostering weren't the kind of kids you contemplated lightly. 'He's a sweetheart,' I reassured him, 'and it's only for a few days while his mum's in hospital.' I then went on to reassure him that, no, Adam *didn't* put her there, and that all being well he'd be gone before they were home again. 'Besides,' I said, 'it'll keep me occupied, won't it? While you and Ty are having your alpine adventure.'

'Adventure?' Mike groaned. 'The only adventure I've had so far is in trying to unbend myself out of that flipping coach seat. I'm as stiff as a board and – sod's law – no sooner do I finally get comfortable enough to nod off than we pull up outside the blinking lodge! Gawd knows where I'm going to find the energy to ski, even after the measly hours' kip we've been granted.'

Tyler, predictably, was bouncing off the ceiling. No, I couldn't see it, but I could hear it in his voice. Though once he'd told me about the coach journey, the Channel Tunnel, the mountains and the snow, he did express regret that I had another child in and he wasn't around to join in.

Which both tickled and moved me. You'd expect – well, I think I would – that a child with Tyler's background would suffer pangs of, if not full-blown jealousy, at least of inse-curity whenever a new child came into our lives. And we had always been braced for it, too. Yet it never happened. I don't know why, and I'd certainly not claim any credit, but there was something about Tyler and how secure he obviously felt with us that let him welcome any new child wholeheartedly.

I wasn't sure why, but my hunch was that it made him feel even more one of us. Part of the fostering 'team'. He was certainly anxious to know all about Adam, and quick to suggest things I might do with him after I'd taken him to see his mum, from the climbing wall at our local leisure centre to a turn on the dry ski slope he'd been on with school.

'Or swimming,' he suggested. 'That's on the way to the hospital.' Which seemed the perfect idea. So I ran with it. Except the next call, to the hospital, brought the dispiriting news that Adam's mum *still* wasn't able to see him.

'It's the medication we had to give her,' the ward sister explained. 'It's an opiate – she's had a lot of pain overnight unfortunately – and it's making her too drowsy to be intelligible.'

'She's all right, though, is she?' I asked, anxious that there might have been some sort of complication.

'Nothing to worry about,' the nurse was quick to reassure me. 'Her vital signs are all fine. She's just in a lot of pain, and we're dealing with it. She'll be right as rain by tomorrow, you'll see. And in a much better place in terms of seeing her little boy. And, truth be told, he'll be much more reassured when he *does* see her than he would be today.'

Which was a fair point. No child likes to see their parent as vulnerable, and if Adam's mum was all over the place (as, with experience of strong painkillers, I knew she probably would be) it made no sense to alarm him unduly. So that was that. When Adam walked sleepily into the kitchen half an hour later it was to hear that yet again he wouldn't be seeing his beloved mother.

He looked distraught, and I could see he was trying to stop himself from crying. 'Mum will be so upset if she doesn't see me soon,' he said, as I hurried to put an arm around him. 'I don't know how she'll cope, I really don't.'

That struck me as a strange thing to say. He reached out as I hugged him and grabbed his painting off the kitchen table, tracing a finger along the arm of the figure on the bed. 'She's going to worry about me,' he added.

'Of course she is, sweetie,' I agreed. 'But she knows you're being looked after …'

'But does she know I'm okay? You know. Not ill or anything?'

'Of course she does,' I lied. There'd been no such conversation. But, then again, why ever would there have been? 'She knows you're fine, that you beat me at chess – two whole times! – and that you're eating me out of house and home. On which note, what d'you fancy for breakfast?'

Quite a lot, as it turned out, once Adam had been reassured. Eggs and bacon, some toast *and* a bowl of cereal. And it struck me that perhaps Adam was a teeny pint-sized athlete, and though I certainly wouldn't be climbing any indoor walls, or falling down any ski slopes, he might relish doing *all* of the activities Tyler had suggested.

Swimming, however, seemed to win the day.

'I love swimming,' he told me. 'We're going with school next term, too. So I need to practise for my 600 metres.'

'Perfect,' I said. 'Swimming it shall be, then.'

Adam frowned. 'But what am I going to do about swimming shorts? The social lady didn't pack any for me.'

'Not a problem,' I reassured him. 'I have quite a selection. We had a boy stay with us for a while a few years back. His name was Spencer. And he was a bit of a water baby too.' I narrowed my eyes. 'Though which football team do you support? Can't have you swimming with the enemy.'

It was the work of moments to establish that Adam had not the least interest in football. Never played it – except sometimes, at school, when he was made to – and had no allegiance to any team. He seemed more interested in Spencer and the whys and wherefores of his stay with us.

'Do you have lots of boys come to stay here?' he asked, once I'd sketched a few details for him.

'I do,' I said, 'and girls. Some for short stays, like you, and some, like my Tyler, who stay with us for a long time.'

'Why?' he asked. Which seemed a reasonable enough question.

'Because not everyone is lucky enough to have a mum who loves them like yours does,' I told him. 'And sometimes, because some mums and dads, for all sorts of reasons, can't look after their children themselves.'

'So is this in care? Me being here?' He looked suddenly anxious.

'Yes, officially, I suppose,' I said. 'But not the way you might have heard of it. I'm simply taking care of you till your mum's better and she can look after you again herself.'

'Does she know about you?' he asked me, as we climbed the stairs to go rummage in my clothes cupboard. 'You know – that you're a proper carer person and I'm safe and that?'

'Of course.'

'That's good,' he said. 'She won't worry so much about me then, will she?'

By then the all-important business of choosing swim shorts was underway, or perhaps I would have pondered that a little more fully.

We spent a lovely morning swimming, and despite my earlier assumption, Adam turned out not to be the athlete I had suspected. In fact, he struggled in the water. It was clear he loved it, however, and was keen to improve, not to mention revelling in the opportunity to go a little wild and splash and scream down the water slides – the ones at the shallow end, normally enjoyed by kids half his age.

I wondered about that as I took a breather on the tiled steps at the pool's edge. About what his head teacher had said about him being a sickly boy. How he had so much time away from school. It didn't quite fit; his low weight and pale features aside, Adam seemed a picture of health. Good appetite, plenty of energy and perfectly sociable, if not apparently generally social. Right now, for instance, he was chatting away with a group of boys whom I suspected he'd never met.

So why the issues, when, by and large, he couldn't have seemed more normal? Was he just the son of a massively overprotective mother, and being social and educationally stifled as a result? It wasn't unheard of, after all, and if she was truly on her own – no partner, no family – perhaps being overprotective of her child was understandable. Perhaps I'd ask him, I thought, as I stood up to go and rejoin him. Or perhaps *not*, I chastised myself as soon as I'd thought it. Nothing to do with me. Not my brief. Not my business.

Still, me being me – someone who rarely listened to chastising voices, my own included – we had barely fastened our seatbelts in the car to set off home when my gentle prying started. I couldn't seem to help myself: the disconnect between the now ruddy-cheeked boy with me and the boy described to me by his head teacher was just too great. 'Do you go swimming with your mum?' I asked, smiling through the rear-view mirror.

He shook his head. I'd bought him a carton of juice and he was busy stabbing at the hole with the straw, and once he'd succeeded and taken a slug he elaborated. 'Mum doesn't really like me going swimming,' he said. 'She worries I might get hurt, or drown or something. Plus there's germs in the changing rooms.'

'There are indeed,' I said, not wishing to appear to disagree with him. 'What about school, though? You're going with school next term, aren't you? Mum okay with that?'

He inclined his head, as if thinking about that. 'Sort of. She has to let me do that because it's in the rules for year six. But if she worries too much she'll just keep me home from school.'

His tone was matter of fact rather than resentful. Accepting rather than questioning. Again, I wondered at his seeming quiet compliance. My senses were enjoying no such pragmatism, however. This surely wasn't right. This was evidence that she was keeping him off school not for his own good but to manage her own anxiety about his safety. In my line of work, the word 'neglect' was very often the key one when it came to parenting, but I had also come across parents who were mildly overprotective, not letting their children play in playgrounds and so on. This seemed a step further on, however.

But not my business. I changed both subject and tack. 'So what about other members of your family,' I asked him chattily. 'D'you have cousins? Uncles and aunties? Any living nearby?'

He shook his head again, but then he smiled. 'I had a granddad,' he explained. 'He was clever, he was. He left me his train set. He built it all himself – buildings and everything. But he died just before I was born, so I never actually met him. And Nanny Pat died when I was six. She had cancer.'

I imagined this little lad, custodian of a train set whose maker he'd never known, but in whose love he clearly basked even so. 'Oh, that's sad,' I said. 'You must miss your nan.'

'Not specially,' Adam told me. 'I never saw her much. I miss Uncle Steve though. He lives in Torremolinos.' The word rolled effortlessly off his tongue.

'Oh, Spain, then,' I said.

'He has a bar there,' Adam told me. 'And a girlfriend – she's called Selina – but we don't see them much. They don't have any kids yet, or else I'd have some cousins.'

'You would indeed,' I agreed. 'So, have you been there? To Torremolinos?'

Adam nodded. 'Only once, when Uncle Steve got engaged. I was nine,' he added helpfully. 'They had this huge outside party. In the bar, with a barbecue. But we only stayed two days. There was a boy who'd got kidnapped – did you know about that?' I nodded. 'In Greece, that was. It happened when mum was younger, and it was all over the papers. She said we couldn't stay, because she kept getting frightened.'

Adam slurped up the rest of his juice and I did a re-jig. Not so much an overprotective mother as an extremely overprotective mother. I wondered what might have happened in her earlier life to make her feel that way. It must be so disabling to be crippled by such chronic anxiety. And the poor woman – she really did seem alone in the world, too. Just one brother. And him so far away. No wonder she came across as a worrier to the school. I was anxious to meet her now, and learn a bit more.

But that was all. Academic interest. No more.

Chapter 3

Sunday

'I've been relegated.' Mike's voice was a picture of perfect misery. No, I couldn't see it, but I could imagine the expression on his face.

It was once again early, and, as Adam was still asleep, I'd called my beloved for an update. 'Relegated?' I asked him, genuinely stumped. 'Relegated from what?'

'From Tyler's ski school class,' he huffed. 'They've moved me down to the bloody debutantes.'

'Debutantes?' I couldn't help but guffaw at this, even as I felt a tinge of pride that Tyler's dry-slope endeavours had paid off. He'd be made up about that, I knew.

'As in beginners,' Mike translated. 'Because I'm too slow, apparently. Holding the group up. Bloody cheek of it! I mean, I know I'm not as slick as some of the others, but honestly, when I am upright I am as fast as the next person. Possibly faster, even. I am deeply offended!'

He wasn't really, of course. This was all for Tyler's bene-fit. I felt certain Mike didn't give a monkey's cuss about it, but he was still going to milk it for all that it was worth.

'Oh, but you should have seen me, Case,' he told me, once Tyler had headed off to breakfast with his group. 'You know that thing they say about skiing being like riding a bike? Well, it's not. I've not only forgotten everything I ever learned. I've even forgotten how to make my legs move backwards and forwards, honest! Oh, you will be *so* glad you didn't come on this. You'd *hate* it. Well, actually, you'd have enjoyed seeing me yesterday – I looked like a prize wally, tumbling head over backside on my first attempt. And my second. And then my third … Still, at least it gave Ty and his mates a good laugh.'

I tried to picture my six-foot-plus husband trying to control a pair of six-foot-plus – or thereabout – planks of slippery wood. And failing. Because I just couldn't visualise it. I could only hope some enterprising soul had got some footage. And said so, which didn't go down well at all.

'Typical. Not a single shred of sympathy,' Mike blus-tered. 'Anyway, how are things with the little lad you're looking after?'

'Fine,' I said. 'Calm,' I said. 'Uneventful,' I elaborated. I didn't need a lecture from Mike, after all.

But there was no doubt that I was as intrigued to meet Mrs Conley – for that was her name – as I knew Adam would be excited. Not that I planned on waking him up and dragging him from his bed just yet. So, after calling my sister Donna to let her know I'd be bringing Adam down to her café for a late Sunday lunch, I was straight on to the hospital again to see how the patient was doing.

'Much better,' the ward sister assured me. 'Her pain's under control and she's altogether brighter. So, yes, please do bring her son up to see her this afternoon. It'll be a tonic for both of them, I'm sure.'

It was certainly a tonic for Adam, who grinned from ear to ear when I told him, then wolfed down his breakfast, almost as if in celebration – or more likely, to be done with it, and help the minutes tick faster till he and his mum could finally be reunited.

And who was I to worry that she seemed to be stifling him? I saw the opposite of that all the time, didn't I? So much better to have a surfeit of love and care than too little, surely? And so what if she smothered him a little, or worried too much? He was a bright, polite boy with the world at his feet. Not everyone was destined to be a roughty-toughty gad-about. The world needed all sorts of people, after all.

You could have fried an egg on my quiet, bookish, sickly house-guest, he was that fired up about the impending hospital visit, growing more and more restless as the clock hands moved slowly round to past twelve. Though he'd been happy enough to watch telly for a bit and then help me with a bit of housework – 'me and Mum do it together, always' – he was becoming increasingly distracted as the morning wore on.

'Come on!' he said as the time came and he jumped into the car ahead of me. He said it again as we were slowed down by Sunday shopping traffic, then again as I rummaged in my bag to find sufficient coins to feed the hospital car park meter, and a fourth time as I waited for my ticket to be dispensed.

'Calm *down*,' I said, placing the ticket on the dashboard. 'Such ants in your pants! It's not even one o'clock yet! And it's not like your mum's going anywhere, is it?'

'But we'll be late,' Adam persisted, refusing to be mollified. 'And if we're late, Mum'll be worried. She'll think something's happened to me.'

'I'm sure she won't,' I told him as he took my hand again, mostly to drag me all the quicker across the car park. 'I'm sure they won't even let us on to the ward yet.'

But he looked genuinely worried, and what he said next confirmed it. 'You don't understand, Casey. She's going to be either *really* annoyed or *really* upset.'

I was about to reassure him that she would most likely just be thrilled to see him, but he got in first. 'Casey, I haven't been ill since I've been with you, have I?'

Another odd question. But I was becoming used to Adam's odd questions. I smiled and squeezed his hand. 'No, darling, you've been perfectly fine. You know that. Now come on, let's go find that ward.'

Though I knew the hospital, I'd never been on Adam's mum's ward before, so it was via the miracle of those coloured routes they paint on hospital floors that we found our way. In this case, it was purple and, as the ward in question was on the ground floor, simply a case of following the line to the open double doors.

'Mandy Conley?" said a young, smiling nurse. 'You'll find her over in that corner bay of beds at the far end of the ward. See?' She pointed. 'And she's much better today, I'm glad to say.' She beamed down at Adam. 'Even ate some lunch.'

The ward did indeed smell of roast dinner and, unusually, it made my tummy rumble. Hospital food must be on the up, I decided.

I thanked the nurse and hurried off, trying to catch up with Adam, who, having let go of my hand, was already hotfooting it off to the far end of the ward. I caught up with him just as he reached the end bay and was running towards her outstretched arms.

Adam's mum had the same angular features as Adam, and her hair, which was long and pulled back into a scrunchie, was the same colour and texture as his. Unlike Adam, however, she was quite an ample woman, which only heightened the intensity of the mother–son union. He threw himself at her, and she quickly engulfed him.

It was a tender scene, the pair of them hugging each other tightly, and I could immediately see how much they had missed each other. In fact, so immersed were they in one another that I felt a little out of place, and uncomfortably as though I were intruding.

Adam's mum caught my eye over him, and she smiled a wan smile. She was very pale – almost grey – and I could see that, despite her obvious pleasure at seeing her son, his tight embrace was making her wince.

She whispered something to him and he let her go, upon which she stuck a hand out. I stepped forward and took it. 'I'm Casey,' I said. 'Casey Watson. Nice to meet you. How are you feeling, Mrs Conley?'

'It's *Mandy*,' she corrected, much as I'd corrected Adam. 'And I'll live, I imagine. I still feel like I've gone ten rounds with Mike Tyson, but' – she smiled – 'good old Mr Morphine helps a *lot*.' She ruffled her son's hair. 'How has Adam been? Has he suffered with his stomach? He's such a little soldier.' She looked at him as if analysing his expression for unexpected turbulence. 'Such a little trouper. He's probably tried to hide it.'

I was a little taken aback, and looked at Adam to try to establish what I might have missed. Yes, I knew what the school had told me – and had at no point forgotten it – but, for all that it had been a fact that had been impressed upon me, it simply hadn't come up. Not once. At no time had Adam so much as gestured towards his stomach – except during the business of filling it.

But had I been wrong? Had my instinct betrayed me? Had Adam been suffering in silence all this time? I looked at him again and I saw him anew. He actually *did* look a little peaky – and his demeanour had changed too. Hard to say how, but something definitely had altered.

But I stated the facts. 'No, he hasn't been unwell,' I told his mother. 'Not as far as I am aware, anyway. You've been fine, haven't you, love?' I said, turning to Adam again.

Adam nodded, his expression grave, as if this were a matter of great importance.

'He really has been *fine*,' I reassured his mum. 'His appetite had been good. Actually, that's something of an understatement. And we've been out and about, we've gone swimming, and though he's obviously missed you a lot, he's been in good spirits.'

Adam's mum, however, appeared not to hear me. Well, bar a brief raise of her eyebrows at the word 'swimming'. It was as if she wasn't listening, so intent was she on carefully looking her child over, smoothing his hair back, feeling his forehead, stroking his cheek. As if suspicious that anyone could possibly look after him properly.

I filed the thought away, beginning to feel almost as if I was intruding on the pair of them. 'Have you got everything you need?' I asked Mrs Conley, gesturing with a hand back up the ward. 'Only I could get you a few bits from the shop in the main reception if you need anything. Toiletries? Snacks? Something to read?'

Mrs Conley – *Mandy* – turned and smiled at me. 'That's kind of you, but I'm fine, thanks. I had a bag prepared at home, so I've already got everything I need. And a trolley comes around every morning, of course. And I'm hoping' – she squeezed Adam's upper arm as she spoke – 'that I'll be home with my little soldier in a day or so. No, no, please' – she gestured – 'grab a seat. I want to hear everything about what my little man has been up to.'

Still I dithered about popping out, wondering if I should leave them for a bit anyway, but Adam seemed anxious that we tell her all about my chess lessons and our swimming trip. But in the end, as the bay opposite was currently empty, I still went and sat on the chair beside it and took out my phone so the two of them could chat more privately. My son Kieron had recently taught me all about Facebook and installed it on my phone, so I now had a whole new virtual world to entertain me.

And distract me from earwigging – nobody is perfect.

And the visit passed quickly enough. Only thing was – and perhaps this was going to be inevitable – that Adam's mood, as we left, dropped like a stone. And in the resultant silence (down and withdrawn, he would not be engaged in conversation) a strange thought popped into my head. What had Mandy said? *I already had a bag prepared.* That was it. But how on earth could she have? I was sure John Fulshaw had told me she had been rushed into hospital with appendicitis, as an emergency. Sure as sure. Her appendix had actually burst, hadn't it?

Okay, I thought – so maybe she was just a very private person and didn't want me to go and buy her personal things. But if so, why not just say 'No, thank you'? Why mention a bag – a prepared bag – at all? Was the appendicitis story not the real one? Was that it? Was there something I wasn't being told?

Stop it, I told myself. Stop being a conspiracy theorist. Who knew? She might have bags packed for all sorts of contingencies. Perhaps her appendix had been grumbling for a while. Perhaps it was all part of the scenario of being an over-anxious person.

That was probably it. Some people stockpiled tins ready for nuclear war, didn't they? And there was nothing I'd seen between her and Adam to concern me. Even were it my business to *be* concerned.

Which it wasn't. And I was at least partially satisfied that I was reading things into things that weren't actually there.

I glanced at Adam. 'You okay, love?' I asked him. 'How's your tummy?'

And there it was. Just the tiniest moment of hesitation. Not as if he wasn't sure how his tummy felt – not at all. No, more that he was deciding *how best* to answer me.

So I wasn't wrong. Something definitely wasn't right.

Chapter 4

Monday

Though he'd perked up at the sight of a roast dinner the previous afternoon, Adam had gone to bed on Sunday night markedly more subdued than he'd been previously – even giving me another chess lesson had failed to enthuse him – and with the prospect of a day at school on the horizon, I wondered how he'd be this morning. Seeing his mum had obviously knocked him for six.

'She's going to be absolutely fine, you know,' I said, as I passed him a bowl of cocoa-dusted cereal. 'In fact, I bet they say she can come home any day now, just you wait and see.'

Adam picked up his spoon and began shovelling the cereal into his mouth. 'I know,' he said, sighing once he'd swallowed a couple of mouthfuls. 'It's just that I worry about her. She's not used to being without me.'

My sense of an unhealthy maternal dependence only deepened. In an ideal world, no child should have to stress in that way about a parent. But we weren't living in an ideal world. He was stressed, and I could only try to help him. 'Well, tonight,' I said briskly, 'we'll be back to see her, okay? We'll come home, have a bit of tea, and then go straight back for another visit. That way, she won't worry so much, will she?' I had another thought. 'And tonight I'm going to take my puzzle book with me, too, so I can sit in the waiting room, and give you and your mum a bit of proper catch-up time. How does that sound?'

Good enough to cheer him up, apparently. He wolfed down the rest of his breakfast, plus the banana I offered him, and even asked what he was getting for his lunch. He'd already told me the previous evening that he didn't 'do' school dinners (wrinkling his nose in the time-honoured fashion, too), so I'd filled a plastic box with the things he said he liked most – a cheese sandwich, some crisps and another banana – while he went back upstairs to clean his teeth and get his bag.

So far, so largely unremarkable. And as I watched him go into school, I made a mental note to put aside all the concerns that had been niggling at me; he was just a little lad, cast adrift, feeling anxious, who was missing both his routine and his mum.

As I was missing all the absentee members of my own family I was feeling more than a little adrift myself. So I wasn't altogether unhappy to hear, when I called John Fulshaw, that, assuming I was okay with it, I'd have Adam with me for a few more days yet.

'They're keeping her in for a bit – just a couple more days, to be on the safe side,' he explained. 'Nothing to worry about – just so they can get her pain under control. Which makes sense, since she's Adam's sole carer.'

I agreed that it did, remembering how grey and weak Adam's mum had looked. No point sending her home if she wasn't going to be able to cope.

'That's absolutely fine,' I said. 'Like I told you, I'd have been at a very loose end this week had it not been for this, so yes, I'm happy. Bless him – he's the sweetest boy. No trouble at all. And bright, too – he's teaching me how to play chess.'

John diplomatically didn't express any surprise at this, but once I'd rung off it did occur to me that it would be an odd sort of week – just Adam and me, bent studiously over various board games.

Generally speaking, I'm not a solitary person. Oh, I enjoy the odd five minutes' peace as much as any frazzled parent, but that was only because it was such a treat. I was used to the proverbial houseful – kids and grandkids and foster kids all coming and going; being in the centre of a whirlwind was much more my *modus operandi* than feeling like a lone tumbleweed rolling across a plain. Which made my thoughts turn again to Adam and his mum's apparent isolation; what different lives they must live to my own. And it had been a contrast that was brought to the fore even more when I called Mike and, because the mobile-phone signal was in and out like a swing door, he seemed such a very long way away.

The day therefore dragged, despite my attacking all the housework, and I found myself a full ten minutes early for pick-up time at Adam's school.

It was a big school – unfamiliar, too, as none of my tribe had gone there – and as I watched the first kids, the infants, spilling out onto their adjacent playground, my thoughts turned automatically to Adam's friends. He'd presumably been here for almost the full eight years now – time enough, surely, for him to have made some close friends, and, perhaps, for his mother to have too.

And, as if on cue, as I scanned the sea of unfamiliar young faces, I spotted him, coming out with another boy, their heads bent and close, in conversation. And as they got nearer, a new thought appeared in my head. I was all too conscious that I was going to have to break the news to Adam that he was unlikely to be able to go home for a few days yet, so how about – in the interests of maintaining some normality – this friend of his could come round to play?

I raised a hand and waved manically till Adam looked up and spotted me, then trotted across to the gate where they'd emerge. And as I did so, I noticed a young woman heading the same way. Could this be the other lad's mother? She had a toddler on her hip, and was also picking up one of the infants and was pointing out the boys as she approached.

My hunch confirmed when the boy Adam was with waved back at her, I decided to take the bull by the horns. 'Hi,' I said, as she hefted the little one on to her other hip.

'I'm Casey. I'm a foster carer.' I gestured towards the approaching boys. 'I'm looking after Adam for a few days till his mum comes out of hospital.'

'Oh, I see,' she said, nodding. 'Verity. Pleased to meet you. Is Adam's mum okay? Harry told me all about it on Friday.'

'She's fine,' I confirmed, nodding. 'We're off to visit her in a bit. It's obviously tough for Adam –'

'I'll bet,' she said. '*Bless* him. The poor love. Can you imagine that? Just having to be packed off to strangers? Not that you're strange, of course –' She laughed. 'Sorry. That came out all wrong, didn't it? But I was saying to my husband, we'd have had him if we'd known. Well, if there was any way ... hey, there, lovely!' She turned to her son. 'How was your day? And how about you, love?' she added to Adam. 'I hear your mum's on the mend. That's good, isn't it?'

Adam nodded and shyly agreed that it was. Then, in one of those moments of synchronised school-gate thinking, Harry's mum beat me to it. 'Tell you what,' she said, even as I was forming the same words, 'why don't you come to tea with us tomorrow? I know you're going to see your mum today.' She glanced at me. 'But how about tomorrow? You and Harry can have a game of football or something in the park afterwards, can't you? Might take your mind off your mum for a bit.'

There was no other word for it – Adam looked morti-fied. 'I can't,' he said immediately, looking up at me, as if for corroboration. 'I'm not allowed ...'

'Course you are, love,' I reassured him. 'Well, as long as your mum says it's okay. And I can't imagine she *wouldn't* … and we can ask her tonight, can't we?'

He looked stricken. And another thought occurred to me. 'We can still visit her tomorrow,' I told him. 'Visiting's till eight, so there's no problem doing both, love. We could go when I pick you up from Harry's.'

'I *can't*,' he said again, and I could see he was close to tears now. And it was that, together with the look on Harry's mum's face – which, interestingly, displayed none of my consternation – that made me realise there was nothing to be gained in pushing it. What did I know, after all, about these two boys' relationship? If he didn't want to go, he didn't want to go, end of.

He'd already turned away and begun marching off – in entirely the wrong direction – so I mouthed a 'sorry' to Harry's mum and hurried after him.

'I thought Harry was your friend?' I said lightly, once I'd caught up with him, walked with him to my car and got in.

'He *is* my friend,' Adam said, his voice tight with anger. 'He's my *best* friend.'

'So how come you didn't want to go to tea with him, love?'

'Because I'm not *allowed*.'

I watched his face in the rear-view mirror. He was staring miserably out of the window. 'Because you're with me?'

'Because I'm not allowed to go to *tea*.'

'What, not at all?' I asked, dampening the surprise in my voice.

He shook his head. 'No. I have to have my tea at home. With my mum.'

I thought back to the expression on Harry's mother's face. Unsurprised. So she must presumably be aware of this house rule. And she'd made that comment. That they'd have had Adam. And then that unfinished qualification that had not gone unnoticed. *If there was any way* ... Was that what she'd meant? If there was any way the apron strings could be loosened a fraction?

So I couldn't help but wonder. And worry. There was close and there was close.

I wondered if his mum realised that – in her loneliness, presumably – she might actually be preventing him from having a normal childhood.

I was all too aware that it wasn't my role to try to probe into Adam's home life but I made another attempt on the journey to the hospital. We'd been talking about his mum and how happy she'd be to see him, and it seemed it couldn't hurt, specially as she was now going to be staying in a few more days. Surely she'd see that it would be good for him to see a school friend in her absence. 'I tell you what,' I said. 'How about I have a chat with your mum, eh? You know, about you going to tea at Harry's tomorrow?'

But the response was, if anything, even more pronounced. 'No!' he snapped. It was the first time he'd raised his voice with me. 'I don't *want* to! Please don't ask Mum about it, Casey. *Please*.'

And that was that. Duly noted. End of conversation. Much as I wanted to, I didn't ask him why.

Adam's mum wasn't where we'd left her. We arrived on the ward to be told she'd been moved into a side room. 'More comfortable for her,' the nurse said. Then, to me, once Adam had skipped off to find her, 'She's not been sleeping well. A bit of pain. She's doing absolutely *fine*,' she added, 'but she's been struggling a bit, so it made the most sense.'

It wasn't for me to ask questions in this situation, so I didn't, but that didn't stop me understanding both the subtext and the nurse's expression – both of which seemed to indicate that Mrs Conley had been moved so that the other patients on the ward could get some sleep.

Again, I filed it away, and when I entered the room I was heartened to see that she was looking brighter and a good deal less pale. And this time, as per my promise, I didn't linger. If it felt intrusive to be close by in the bay on the main ward, it felt doubly so in the cramped side room she now occupied. Plus there was only one chair, which was right by the bed, so, after saying hello and pulling a book of Sudoku puzzles from my handbag, I explained that I'd go down and sit in the hospital café, and return to collect Adam in an hour.

Though once I got to the café, which was chock full of people, I abandoned the puzzle book within a matter of minutes, not least due to my inability to complete one. Instead I called Mike, who'd just returned to the lodge they were staying in. He was full – as people on adventurous holidays usually are – of the snow and the sun and the fun of it all, and made solicitous enquiries about whether I was bored to tears.

'How's the little lad doing?' he asked. 'Not too upset to be stuck with you for longer?'

I'd texted him this news earlier in the day. 'On the contrary,' I told him, 'though he's obviously missing his mum. I'm at the hospital now, as it happens, killing time while he visits her. Then it's home for tea and no doubt another game of chess. But what about you? What about Tyler? I've texted him twice today and heard nothing.'

'I'm not surprised, Case, he's loving it. Absolutely adores it. And he's so good. It's like he was born to ski, it really is.'

'Steady on. Last time I looked he didn't have a mouthful of silver spoons, love.'

'No, but seriously. I've been thinking. We could do this if we saved up. You know – next winter. Make it our next big holiday. Because I'm loving it too. And …'

And on he went, and I think I made all the correct responses, though, in truth, I shuddered at the thought. My choice of holiday attire tended towards bikinis, sarongs and flip flops – not enormous fleecy snow suits and giant boots.

Still, we'd see, and after speaking to Tyler I decided not to rule it out. He really was *so* full of it, and why wouldn't he be? He was a sporty teenage boy. And more importantly, I knew his younger brother – still with their biological father – got treated to all kinds of exotic holidays.

So, well, maybe. For Tyler. Somewhere sunny and not too cold. It was only when I put the phone down that it struck me that the pair of them were in cahoots, which at least put a smile on my face as I hurried back to collect Adam.

He already had his coat on when I arrived and seemed in much better spirits, and his mum looked in good spirits too. And though I still wondered if I shouldn't send him out on some spurious errand so I could ask his mum about his friend Harry, I opted not to. Their arrangements re teatimes were none of my business – I could almost hear Mike saying exactly that in my ear. So instead I led him out, with a promise that we'd return the following teatime, and resolved that we'd say no more about it.

And it seemed as though Adam had very little to say himself. Once again he seemed preoccupied and barely spoke on the journey home. And then, even more curiously, he said he didn't want anything to eat – the first time he'd refused food since he'd come to me.

'Are you sure?' I said. We'd only had a snack before going to the hospital, after all. 'Or did you have something to eat with your mum?'

It seemed unlikely. Hospitals didn't generally extend to feeding visitors, and I doubted his mum, with no other visitors, would have any contraband.

He shook his head. 'I just don't feel like anything, that's all.'

I felt his forehead, automatically. 'How are you feeling in yourself?' I said. 'Does your tummy hurt?'

This time he shook his head emphatically. 'I'm just tired,' he said. 'Is it all right if I go to bed?'

At Risk

'What, at this time?' I asked him. It wasn't even seven. Then, 'Of course. If you want to. If you're not feeling yourself. Shall I come up and tuck you in?' No, he didn't want me to do that. 'Then I'll pop up in a bit and see how you're doing. How about that? If you're feeling better, I can easily make you something then.'

This seemed to satisfy him, and he headed off upstairs, leaving me with little to do bar prepare my own tea and, while doing so, to reflect that he'd had a stressful few days. And that even if stress wasn't making him feel poorly, it was possible that he'd picked up a tummy bug in school. Happily, however, when I checked on him before eating, he was tucked up in bed, sound asleep.

Left to my own devices at an unexpectedly early hour, I decided that, after writing up my daily report, I would spend the evening in my pyjamas, watching the soaps and then perhaps a movie. It was only rarely that I did this, mainly because Mike and Tyler liked their own programmes – which I didn't mind, because I was usually one for pottering in the evenings: sorting uniforms and work clothes, making up lunches for the following day and generally not sitting down for very long. But tonight, for a change, I decided I would be a couch potato and, since there was nothing on, film-wise, that I fancied staying up for, I decided I would treat myself to an episode of *CSI*.

I'd just pressed 'play' when I heard footsteps on the landing. At first I didn't jump up because there seemed to be no need to. Simply Adam, having woken up and headed for the loo. Still, I listened, because he might well be on his way downstairs, and when that didn't happen, and no flush happened either, I pressed 'pause' and headed upstairs to see if he was okay. And halfway up the stairs I realised he was being sick.

Bless him. No wonder he'd been so pale and tired-looking, brewing one of those bugs primary schools tend to incubate, and which go round the pupils like wildfire. I reached the top of the stairs and knocked on the bathroom door. 'Sweetheart?' I called, over a second bout of retching. 'You okay? Can I come in?'

I turned the handle anyway. But it was locked, leaving me unable to do much, though moments later I heard the toilet flush and the bolt being slid back, then Adam appeared, holding his glasses in one hand and a tissue to his mouth. 'Oh, bless you,' I said. 'No wonder you didn't want anything to eat. How are you feeling now? Any better for getting it all out?'

Adam wiped his mouth with the tissue, and a bunch of clammy hair from his forehead. 'I'm okay now,' he said. 'I just felt really, really funny. But I'm okay now I've been sick.'

'I'm sure you are,' I reassured him, though privately I doubted it. Stomach bugs were notorious for lulling you into a false sense of security then sneaking up on you a second time. Which was why I didn't offer him anything to eat. 'Well, you hop back into bed,' I told him, 'and I'll go down and fetch you a glass of water. Though only sips, okay? Give your tummy a chance to settle.'

But when I returned with it, the instruction had been pointless anyway, because Adam was once again fast asleep.

And he remained so for the rest of the evening. Despite my near certainty that there would be another bout of vomiting before he was clear of it, the bug, if bug it was, didn't trouble him again.

Which allowed a new thought to worm its way into my brain. Perhaps it hadn't been a bug. Perhaps it had just been anxiety. After all, I hadn't actually *seen* any sick, had I? Perhaps he was just suffering extreme nausea due to separation anxiety – perhaps being away from his mum was affecting him in unexpected ways. Perhaps there was something in the business of his reported 'weak stomach'. Perhaps, after all, I had been barking up the wrong tree, and his not being allowed to go to tea with school friends was all wrapped up in some ongoing *mental* health issues – which might or might not be related to the somewhat stiflingly close (to my mind, at any rate) relationship he had with his mother. It wasn't unheard of, after all.

Which round of thinking, mostly conducted as I lay awake in the small hours listening for sounds from across the landing, only served to remind me that, when it came to hearts and minds, nothing was simple. Almost every situation was complex and multi-factorial, and though I was in no way qualified to make any kinds of assumptions, I should at least note my thoughts down for John. After all, in the absence of background problems or otherwise, perhaps this little family would benefit from some input from social services, after all.

Chapter 5

Tuesday

Adam was up and about before I was the following morning – perhaps unsurprisingly, since he'd slept for so long. And was apparently fine, batting away my concerns about his sickness and assuring me that what he mostly was was starving.

'I'm not surprised,' I said, feeling reassured by both his colour and his demeanour that it was safe enough to take him to school. 'Though let's go easy, eh?' I added, watching him wolf down his breakfast. 'Don't want you getting sick all over again, do we?'

'I'm fine, honest, Casey,' he told me between mouthfuls. 'It's probably just my weak stomach. I've been to the doctor's lots about it. Didn't they tell you?'

By 'they' I presumed he meant either his teachers or social services. And, given I wasn't fully convinced he'd been physically sick just now, it prompted me to ask him a question.

'Are you often sick, then, love? You know, randomly, like last night?'

He shook his head. 'I have been. Not lots, but sometimes. Mum's had me up the doctor's, like I said, but they don't know what's wrong with me. That's why I have to be careful what I eat.'

Curiouser and curiouser. On the one hand he's sick with some mystery stomach ailment, I thought, and on the other he's chowing down Coco Pops. Careful what he ate?

I had a feeling I could strap a feed bag to his head and fill it with *anything*, and this lad would eat it.

It made no sense. Nothing about Adam seemed to make sense. 'Come on, then,' I said. 'Breakfast time over. Run up and clean your teeth, and then let's hit the road.'

Adam was chatty all the way to school, full of the highs and lows of the day ahead. It was Tuesday, which was good because it meant they had an art session, but on the downside they also had a test for their exams. Best of all, though, was apparently what I'd packed into his lunchbox, which – he'd already hauled it out of his bag and checked – was a four-finger Kit Kat, as a treat. 'That's, like, *mental*!' he'd enthused, which, as I waved him off, struck me as one of the most normal 'boy' things he'd yet come out with. What a strange, isolated life he clearly lived that a chocolate bar could create so much buzz.

As had I, it seemed – a new face at the school gates invariably did – because just as I turned to walk back to my car I saw Harry's mum, Verity, waving at me. She came over, her two-year-old grizzling and wriggling on her hip. It was a little girl, and she reminded me of my granddaughter Marley Mae. Put her down and she'd be off like a shot.

'Any luck?' Verity wanted to know.

I shook my head. 'No, sorry.'

'Such a shame,' she said. Then, without preamble, 'What's *wrong* with her?'

I could have answered that, readily – with questions rather than answers, though it was definitely not my place to pass comment. But it seemed I wasn't going to need to, in any case.

'I honestly don't know,' I said. 'I've only met her – Adam's mother – twice. And to be frank, I didn't ask her. Adam asked me not to.'

Verity rolled her eyes. 'I don't know,' she said. 'People, eh?'

I wasn't sure how to respond to that. But, again, there was no pregnant pause in our conversation, as Verity went on to tell me that Harry was relatively new to the school – they'd only moved to the area the previous autumn. And it seemed she was thrilled by the friendship he and Adam had struck up, because, to use her words, the two of them were 'two peas in the pod', both slight misfits, untroubled by the joys of popularity, and how sad she was that Adam's mum seemed so reluctant to let her child go round to play.

I sympathised, thinking of Kieron, as I naturally would, remembering how much he'd struggled at primary school.

It must be tough for poor Harry, having a whole new world to navigate – tough for his mum too, I didn't doubt.

'Have you met her yourself?' I asked her.

'Barely,' she said. 'She's not what you'd call sociable –' She gestured around us, where wisps of chit-chat floated on the air above various pockets of mums and other carers. The school gates were one of the most social places I knew. 'She never speaks to anyone – just grabs Adam and hurries off. That's when he's in school, of course. She has him off almost as much as she sends him in.'

'So he does get ill then?' I couldn't help but ask, thinking of his episode the previous evening. That and the confounding business of him eating like a particularly hungry horse.

Verity leaned forward conspiratorially. 'According to some of the other mums, he isn't ill at all. Some say that it's been that long since she had a man in her life that she just keeps the poor lad home for a bit of company.' She narrowed her eyes. 'All a bit Norman Bates, if you ask me.'

I shuddered at that thought, but at the same time I couldn't help but laugh. 'Oh dear,' I said. 'The gossip train is on form, then!'

Verity shifted her disconsolate daughter on her hip and sighed a world-weary sigh. 'And hurrah for that,' she said, with feeling. 'Only fun I ever get.'

Once I'd climbed back into my car I noticed Verity had joined another group of mothers – no doubt to fill *them* in on who *I* was, now, as well. Still, that was fine – in return, she'd given me plenty of food for thought. In fact, if the gossip was only half true, it painted quite a sad picture of Adam's life. If he did get genuinely ill, or had a 'sensitive' tummy, then it couldn't be much fun for him or his mum to have such assumptions made. And if it was true – that she was keeping him off school for her own, selfish, purposes, then that was just as bad, if not worse. Either way, the seeds of doubt I'd sown now appeared to be sprouting. I couldn't imagine that he was living a normal childhood.

After going for lunch to my sister Donna's café, and having a catch-up – and yes, a gossip – I spent the rest of the time left before going to collect Adam in doing the laundry and changing various sheets. And I wondered how it must be to be Adam's mother – how I'd feel if I was plopped into a life a bit like hers. Yes, she went out to work, apparently – a care home, John had said, hadn't he? But how must it feel to be in a family of just two? Just him and her. No one else, either to call on, or to help out. I found it hard to imagine, because I'd barely managed half a week and the walls of the house were closing in on me.

So it was in a thoughtful mood that I collected Adam and took him to the hospital, this time via tea at a burger joint en route, which excited him greatly – junk food, yes, but I felt a powerful need to treat him. Then, having left him with his mum, who said she was feeling much better, I went down to the hospital café to call Mike.

But no luck. Mike's phone just kept going straight to voicemail. So, having left a message, I settled instead for a coffee and a jam doughnut and a leaf through a women's magazine, till it was time to collect Adam and take him home again.

It was 3.30 a.m. when I heard Adam being sick again. I knew because the alarm clock was the first thing I saw when the sound of retching jolted me awake. It had been an uneventful evening, Adam once again seeming subdued when I took him home, and keen to do his homework – just some reading – and head straight to bed.

I'd slept fitfully again myself, my mind too full of questions, and Verity's words still very much to the fore. I'd written up my report and sent it, but I'd stopped short of sharing the bulk of my thoughts with John, unsubstantiated as my worries all were. I was also miffed – not to say anxious – that I hadn't heard from Mike yet. It wasn't like the Alps were on the moon, after all. And though I had an emergency number on the sheet from school, I was reluctant to try it – had something happened I knew they would call and tell me.

I pushed back the covers, grabbed my dressing gown and hurried to the bathroom, the door of which this time was at least still ajar. 'Are you all right, love?' I asked Adam, hurrying to kneel down and comfort him as, on his knees, he was hugging the toilet, his glasses abandoned on the bathroom floor.

He raised a hand, as if to stop me from getting too close, and I settled on sitting on the side of the bath instead, while he heaved and retched into the toilet bowl. It must be a bug, surely, or – and I felt a pang of guilt – maybe he really couldn't stomach the rich food he'd eaten. He finally finished, breathing heavily as he reached for the loo roll, and I wondered if I should perhaps call out the doctor.

But when I voiced my concern he was adamant he would be fine – which, again, was something quite outside my experience. No child of his age that I'd ever previously come across took the business of being sick with such apparent unconcern.

Still, he was happy enough to be led back to his bedroom and submitted readily enough to my taking his temperature, which was normal. Once again I tried to get my head round the idea that he really was just a sickly little boy. But sick with *what*? Nothing quite seemed to fit. Adam really was a puzzle – he looked weak and unhealthy, yet he ate really well and had plenty of energy. So what was going on? I really couldn't fathom it.

I stayed with him till he fell asleep again, and again I couldn't settle. Just what was *wrong* with this boy?

Chapter 6

Wednesday

I had already decided it would be best to keep Adam off school for the day, so I didn't wake him up in the morning and crept around the house quietly so as not to disturb him. I was therefore surprised when he bounded into the kitchen, at 7.30 a.m., all smiles and already in his school uniform.

'Morning!' he greeted me. 'What's for breakfast? I'm *starving*.'

I immediately went to feel his forehead, which was neither hot nor clammy. 'Are you sure, love?' I asked, still concerned that he really might have some bug. 'I was going to let you have the day off because you were so sick last night. You might be better off resting up for the day. We could watch TV and just chill out if you like.'

I was half-hoping he would choose this option for selfish reasons too, as I had barely slept at all and felt shattered. But apparently he had other ideas. 'Oh please, no,' Adam said, his face dropping markedly. 'Please don't make me stay home, Casey. It's not fair. I feel fine,' he added. 'Really. I *promise*.'

And he looked it and seemed it. Curiouser and curiouser. 'Adam, it's okay, sweetie,' I said, concerned not only at his crumpled expression but also at what sounded like fear in his voice. 'I wouldn't make you stay at home if you didn't want to. Of course not. Not if you're feeling okay. I just wanted you to know that you *can* have the day off. That was quite a broken night you had there.'

He visibly relaxed, which made me wonder if similar conversations happened regularly in his day-to-day life. Was every school day a battle between mother and son? But why? Since she worked, didn't she *need* him to go to school?

He plonked himself down at the table. 'Thank you,' he said. 'It's just that it's almost end of term today, and I don't want to miss out. Specially not today. We're having an Easter egg hunt.'

I smiled as I opened the fridge. 'Well, in that case, of course you must go. So long as you save me some chocolate if you find any. Deal?'

Adam grinned. 'Deal.'

'So, how about an egg for breakfast too, now, since you're starving?'

He nodded. 'Can I have two?'

Still nothing wrong with his appetite, I noted.

Some gentle probing on the way to school revealed that, as I already knew, Adam didn't like being kept off school, and, as I suspected, he was frequently made to. 'Mum keeps me home all the time,' he said, his tone betraying a rare glimpse of exasperation. 'Even when I ask her not to.'

'Because you've been sick?'

'Not actually sick-sick. That's only sometimes. Just because of my tummy. But I'm *always* okay the next day.' I heard him sigh. 'It's only when I *don't* go to school that I stay sick. 'Cos I get upset, because I'm lonely – and then mum says I set my dicky tummy off all over again.'

I dropped Adam off, feeling desperately sorry for him – a feeling only heightened by his obvious joy at being reunited with his friend Harry. And the feeling soon resolved itself into anger. What the hell was *wrong* with some parents? Here was a perfectly well-behaved, seemingly balanced little boy, and his mother – problems of her own or not – was emotionally suffocating him.

I decided I would stop holding back from interfering. This was clearly a relationship out of kilter. And, quite apart from the emotional toll it seemed to be taking, all these absences meant he was missing out on education.

No, I'd email John again, share my misgivings, and the disclosures Adam had made to me. Hopefully, he would feel them of sufficient importance that he'd have a word with Adam's social worker and suggest some intervention. And who knew? Perhaps Mandy was so wrapped up in her own problems that she didn't even realise she wasn't doing right by her child. Perhaps if she was told – in a gentle, supportive tone – she might learn to let him go a little. No, some family therapy, I thought, could definitely be of value.

And my feelings were only strengthened when, later that afternoon, once I'd collected Adam from school again, Kieron and Lauren popped by with Dee Dee and a bag full of booty. They too were taking off for the Easter holidays, early the following morning, but wanted to drop Easter eggs off for Riley's kids and Tyler before they left. And, sweetly, knowing Adam was staying with me temporarily, they'd even brought an egg for him as well.

'Hope you like chocolate, mate,' Kieron said as he handed it over. It was a huge egg, and caused Adam's eyes to grow in consternation. 'Because I think there's a bunch more chocolate inside there as well.'

'Are you *kidding*?' I asked, eyebrows raised, as I ruffled Adam's hair. 'I haven't found anything this boy doesn't like yet!'

Adam was almost stunned into speechlessness. 'Wow!' he managed eventually. 'This is really all for me?'

'Long as you manage to hold onto it, mate,' Kieron told him. 'Which might not be guaranteed with this menace around.'

We all looked down at Dee Dee, who, oblivious to the bad-mouthing going on around her, was sitting in her pushchair, innocently playing with her favourite ragdoll.

'Can I play with her?' Adam asked. It was a question that surprised me. After all, as far as we knew, he didn't have any little ones in his life. But perhaps that was why.

'I'm a reading buddy,' he said, as Lauren unstrapped her. 'I'm good at reading. I'm in the top set, and once a week I go and read with the reception class.'

'Well, I never,' I said. 'Good for you. Though I can't say I'm surprised. Adam here's a clever lad,' I explained to Kieron and Lauren. 'He's teaching me chess.' To which Kieron politely refrained from guffawing or making some crack about impossible tasks.

Kieron and Lauren didn't stay long – they had a pre-dawn start to drive to the Lake District in the morning, but all the while they were there I found myself mesmerised by Adam and Dee Dee. Which once again fuelled my anger – surely his mum could see how much richer his young life would be if he was allowed more interaction with other children?

So irritated was I by Mandy and all I now knew that when we arrived at the hospital an hour or so later, it was a real effort of will to act as if everything was okay. Specially as the first and only conversation between us consisted of a run-down of how grim she'd been feeling and how useless the nursing staff were.

So I didn't linger, heading straight off to the café once more, where I bumped into the nurse I'd first spoken to on the Monday.

'Becoming your second home, this,' she observed, as I joined her in the queue.

'A bit,' I agreed. 'Though it's only for a few days. And it could be worse. As hospital coffee goes, this is in the Premier League – it's almost drinkable.'

'It's warm and wet – and in a good way, unlike lots of things I have to deal with. You get used to it. Though in your case, here's hoping you don't have to. Mrs Conley should be discharged in a couple of days.'

I told her that was what I'd heard, but that she'd told me she'd been feeling pretty poorly, and the nurse pulled an unmistakable face.

Then shook her head. 'She's doing fine. She's a bit of an odd one, is that one, between you and me.' Then she corrected herself. It wasn't her place to gossip either. 'No, she's recovered well. Don't you worry. They'll discharge her.'

More food for thought, to go with my flapjack. Which I was just biting into when I heard my phone vibrate. Was that an evolutionary development, I found myself wondering, as I put the cake down to fish it out – that, in a world where people were endlessly exhorted to switch their phones off, we'd evolved the power to actually hear vibration?

It took me a while – my handbag being one to rival Mary Poppins' – so by the time I'd located it, whoever had called – my husband hopefully – had already rung off. But pressing the home button revealed that I hadn't missed a call. It was a text – including a video – from Tyler.

Trying to ignore the urge to huff about the probable expense of such a missive, I read the text, and was richly rewarded.

Dad dropped his phone and it won't work. Soz. Was sposed to text you yesterday but it didn't go through. Anyhoo – I don't think his legs will either after this!!!!! The message ended with the now obligatory row of kisses, followed by a video that I had to click to play.

And, to my delight, Tyler had captured the moment perfectly. Goodness only knew how many videos he'd had to record to capture this gem of a mini-film. It was of Mike, setting off skiing – down a ridiculously steep run by the look of it – then risking a wave and paying a pretty heavy price. Head over backside, or backside over head – all detail was lost in a blur of limbs and poles and snow, as he careered off and ended up hugging a tree.

No wonder his mobile was broken.

I headed back to the ward in high spirits – that would learn him. And hopefully scotch any ideas for a skiing break that included me. But I was surprised, when I got onto the ward, to see Adam already emerging from his mum's room and taking care to shut the door very softly.

'Oh, sorry, love,' I said, confused. 'Am I late?'

Adam shook his head. 'No, it's just that Mum's feeling a bit sleepy, so I thought I'd leave her in peace.'

So, what? Dismissed? Or perhaps a disagreement? Had he been telling her about his Easter egg bonanza and got a ticking off? He was definitely looking a bit subdued. 'All right, love,' I said. 'I'll just pop my head in and say good-bye, then, okay?'

Adam nodded. 'Okay,' he said. 'I'll just wait here.' Which made me feel even surer some words must have passed between them.

I opened the door, to find Adam's mum indeed looking sleepy.

'Oh, hello,' she said. 'Sorry, I'm all of a fog. Can't keep my eyes open. I had to have my meds upped because I've been in so much pain. Knocked me for six.'

'Oh dear,' I said, remembering what the nurse had said to me earlier. 'I thought you were doing so well.'

She looked at me sharply. 'Who told you that? Honestly – they'd throw you out on your ear, this lot. Anything to free up a bed. The sister, was it? Honestly, the left arm doesn't know what the right one is doing here! I've seen that many different doctors and nurses, I'm surprised they even know my name.'

I didn't know what to say to that, so managed only a 'yes, well', before she continued, albeit in a slightly softer vein. 'I probably *am* recovering just fine. But it's all about pain control, isn't it? It's just the morning nurse forgot to give me my tablets, and then by the time the lunchtime shift came on I was in agony, of course. They're just kicking in now. As you can see.' She smoothed the covers down. 'Anyway, thank you. I hope Adam's okay.'

'I'm sure he'll be fine,' I assured her.

Adam didn't seem to want to talk during the journey home so I didn't press it. Besides, what his mother had said did make some kind of sense. If she had only just been given her meds and they were strong, then she would feel like that, and there was nothing to be done about it.

But I was distracted from my musings by a sound from

the back seat. Adam was retching again. I immediately pulled the car over and jumped out, but too late. Adam had vomited all over the back seat of the car. I opened the back door anyway and helped him clamber out, where he was promptly sick again all over the side of the road.

'Oh, sweetheart,' I said, as he continued to retch. 'I'm beginning to think we need to get you to the doctor's, love.'

'I'm all right,' Adam insisted, spitting a bit from his mouth.

'No, you're not. It's not right you being sick like this all the time. Even if you do feel okay after you stop.'

He certainly didn't look better. He looked ashen.

'No, you need the doctor's,' I told him, though even as I said it I realised the impracticality of re-routing all the way to our local surgery. It was hardly going to be helpful to pitch up at a busy afternoon surgery, and this was hardly a situation that required us to rush to A&E either. He was already getting his colour back and looking better.

'Well, home then,' I said. 'And then I'm going to ring the doctor. Come on,' I added, looking miserably into the fetid back seat. 'Into the front, then. We'll get you back and cleaned up at least.'

He climbed into the front seat and strapped himself in. At least little had gone over his clothes. 'I'm so sorry,' he said. 'I don't know why this keeps happening.'

Neither did I – I really couldn't make head nor tail of it. But it seemed I was soon to find out.

I ran a bath as soon as we got in, and while Adam had a soak, I went outside, tooled up with rubber gloves, disinfectant and an old T-shirt to use as a disposable cloth, and set about trying to clean my car.

And that's when I saw it. Saw something. What was it? A pink Smartie? My thoughts went immediately to the Easter egg. No, it couldn't be that – I knew he hadn't even opened Kieron's Easter egg. I picked it up gingerly. No, not a Smartie. It was a pill of some sort.

My thoughts then flew, with a jolt, to my medicine box. My *locked* medicine box. In the cupboard in the kitchen. Could I have left it unlocked? Surely not. It was too automatic. Years of training. I'd have never left it unlocked.

I looked closer, holding my nose, and other shapes started to reveal themselves. Shards of pink. Other pieces of tablet as well. Recoiling a little, I scooped the sick out as best I could, scraping what I could into a plastic bag, bound for the dustbin. I then disinfected all the wet areas and finally closed the door, leaving the back window open a bit to help dry it out. Then took stock. What the hell was going on?

I went upstairs to where Adam was just getting into his pyjamas. And asked him straight out if he could tell me what was going on. And he looked at me, at first warily. Then blankly. Too blankly. He had no idea. No, he hadn't taken anything he shouldn't. He didn't know what I was talking about. He'd just been sick, and now he was feeling better. He didn't *know*.

And there was no point in interrogating him further, I knew. So I tucked him in, went downstairs, and I wondered. What should I do now? No Mike to talk it over with, and it was too late to call John Fulshaw. And though I knew I could call the emergency duty team, I didn't. They were chronically stressed, and this wasn't an emergency. What exactly, at this hour, could or should they do?

But something was nagging at me – nudging forcefully at my consciousness. I didn't know what, but I needed to get on the internet. And there, my vague hunch resolved itself into something more concrete. And if I was right – and I hoped I wasn't – this short, simple placement was about to turn into something that wasn't simple at all.

Chapter 7

Thursday

I was on a mission from the minute I got up the next day.
A grim mission, too – the potential implications of which
hardly bore thinking about. I decided to give Adam another
opportunity to tell me what was going on over breakfast, by
asking him if there was anything at all he wanted to talk
about. There wasn't. In fact, it was clear that he'd rather
discuss anything but. Which only added fuel to the fire, not
to mention my anguish at the way things might soon start
unravelling. So after joining him for beans on toast (at his
request, and with me feeling I was feeding a hearty breakfast to the mythical 'condemned man') I dropped him off at
school as usual, then rushed straight back home to make
the phone calls I had been waiting all night to make.

I had searched long and hard, my ideas forming and
changing as I read – I had that infuriating 'tip of the tongue'
thing going on, because I knew I knew something of what
might be going on with Adam but, infuriatingly, couldn't

pin down a name for it. But, of course, as soon as I saw it – outrageous though it seemed – my instinct was as strong as it had ever been. And the more I read, and the more search words I fed into my laptop, the more convinced I became that I knew what we were looking at – a variant of something called Munchausen Syndrome, a psychiatric disorder in which sufferers feign illness to get attention, spending all their time at the doctor's with imagined illnesses, and even getting themselves admitted to hospital. Adam's picture, I thought. Was this what was going on here?

That was chilling enough, but in this case it was Adam who was being affected too; if I was right, his mother might also have Munchausen Syndrome by Proxy (or MBP) in which sufferers feign symptoms of illness in children in their care, again, to get attention – and in some cases (in this case?) actually cause them.

Was that it? Was Adam's mum actually poisoning him? I had heard of Munchausen's, of course. It had come up as part of our fostering training. And I had seen films and news stories about it. But I had never personally encountered it. I shuddered again as I thought about the implications. Was it *really* possible that Mandy Conley had actually been poisoning her own son? Drugging him to make him sick so that she had 'proof' that Adam really was unwell?

I had been up half the night reading about different forms of the disorder, and it didn't make for pleasant bedtime reading. I read of mothers who had poisoned their newborn babies with doctored milk, and of others who had gone so far as to cause physical accidents so that their children would actually break limbs. And all of this so that they could spend even more time at the GP's or in hospital, getting attention, getting solace, being cared for. And the more I read, the more ghoulish and tragic it all seemed. What a complicated thing the human brain was.

And very quickly it all began to make sense. Keeping Adam out of school, keeping him close and not allowing him to socialise, the vomiting – had she been slipping pills to him under my and the nurses' noses? How I regretted those trips to the café. The fear of germs, the business of Adam not being allowed to eat in other children's houses – all part of the elaborate construction, created, if I was right, by a severe and dangerous mental illness.

Or was I the mad one, barking up completely the wrong tree?

'No, you're not mad,' John Fulshaw reassured me, after I'd gone on in this vein for a full five minutes on the phone to him. 'In fact, *wow*. Though I can't quite believe it myself, I fear you might just have hit the nail on the head.'

I was relieved that he'd read my emails and seemed to think I was right. 'But what do I *do*, John?' I said. 'I mean, what do *we* do? Confront the mother? Call the police? Get in touch with Adam's social worker? That would be the first thing, I suppose. Share this, pronto.'

'Well, in theory, yes,' John said, 'except that Adam doesn't actually have an assigned worker, as such. These were very different circumstances, obviously. But now, in light of the evidence – the pills in his sick, particularly – we have no choice. Leave it with me for now. I'll get on the phone and speak to the manager of Adam's local team, and we'll work out a plan of action. In the meantime, you'll just have to sit tight I'm afraid, Casey.'

'What about tonight's visit?' I asked, concerned. 'Should I stay in the room with them this time?'

'Oh, you can't take him tonight, Casey,' John said. 'Not now all this has come to light. There's no way we can allow him to go back, so you'll just have to come up with something. You can do that, can't you? If it's true, and she does suffer from MBP, then she needs help – and fast.'

'You do agree it's probably that, then?'

'I sincerely hope so. Because if it's not that, then it's something even more sinister, isn't it? Which means it'll be up to the police and the courts to decide what happens next, won't it? But definitely no to taking him back there, okay?'

I felt sick myself as I put the phone down. I wasn't someone who generally felt stress in my stomach, but I really did feel nauseous thinking about the enormity of it all. That poor little boy, and now, if what I knew to be true in my gut *was* really true, he was probably going to lose his mother, at least in the short term. And what was that kind of trauma going to do to him?

I tried to keep a calm head on my shoulders – for heaven's sake, I'd dealt with enough horrible abuse situations to be able to deal with this, surely. But there was just something so eerie and disconcerting about this one. I don't know why – all forms of child abuse were horrible and shocking – but it was perhaps just the realisation that, had Adam's mother not had her appendicitis, she might well have continued harming Adam for years. Might even have killed him.

I was still a bit shell-shocked when I picked Adam up from school later in the day. And I hated that I was going to have to lie to him. All the way home I kept thinking about how his whole world was about to implode – truly implode now, not just be interrupted – and it was almost a relief when he started to get angry that he couldn't visit his mum, and demanded to know why. Having to concentrate on the confection of falsehoods I'd had to peddle at least gave me something to do.

'I told you, sweetie,' I repeated, when he refused to accept it. 'There's some kind of bug going around the ward – everybody's got it. One of those superbugs they're always talking about on the news. So all visits have been cancelled. No exceptions. Even for us, sorry. I know it's tough, but let's just wait and see how things are tomorrow, hey?'

Adam eyed me suspiciously – as I knew he probably would. After all, it takes one to know one. Then he frowned, and I could see he was thinking about something. 'Hang on,' he said slowly. 'Is that really true, Casey?' I felt skewered by the intelligence of his stare. 'You thought *I* had a bug, didn't you?' he went on. 'Is that why I can't go? Because you think *I* have a bug, and I might make Mum ill?'

He paused, as if weighing up what, if anything, to say next. I let the pause expand. Seeing his expression, I had no interest in filling it.

And my hunch that there was something coming was rewarded. 'Because if that's the reason,' he said eventually, 'it's all right. You *can* take me. I don't have a bug. I was sick because of the pills. I worked it out. It was just the wrong medicine.'

'The wrong medicine? You've been taking medicine, Adam?'

He nodded. 'But it wasn't the same as my normal medicine. It wasn't the same colour as the ones I normally have. *That's* why I was sick. I worked it out. At least, I think so.'

There. He'd said it.

I was stunned into silence for a moment, but then the training kicked in. I had to be really careful about how I questioned Adam, and would also have to try to remember every single word of this conversation. 'So it was your mum who gave you those pills yesterday, love?' Adam nodded. 'And you're telling me that you always get given pills?' Another nod. 'But different ones?'

'Yes, white ones,' he answered quietly. 'To keep me well. I have to.' His eyes were searching mine now, as if for some evidence that I could be trusted. That I believed him. 'If I don't take my pills every day I could get properly sick,' he went on. 'And my mum doesn't want me to die.'

And was slowly killing him. I forced the thought away. Steady *on*. But something in my expression – probably that – had clearly frightened Adam. He was looking increasingly anxious, and he now touched my arm. 'Casey, what will happen now I've told?'

I knelt down in front of where he stood, his eyes full of tears now, put my arms out to him and pulled him in for a hug. I had to be honest here. No lies. No platitudes. 'Baby, I really don't know,' I said. What else could I say? The one thing I couldn't do was reassure him that things would be okay, because I was quite, quite sure that they wouldn't be. Not in the immediate future, anyway. 'But it was right for you to tell me. It truly was.' I released him sufficiently that I could look into his eyes again. 'What I can tell you is that children who are not ill shouldn't be given tablets. It's the tablets that have been making you sick, sweetie. Not the other way around.'

Adam was 11, and bright, and his answering nod confirmed that he'd already worked that out. Some time ago, probably, but what do you do when you are 11, and your mum, whom you loved, and was your only source of love and security, tells you repeatedly that white is black?

Adam pulled off his glasses and scraped the back of his hand across his eyes. 'Can't you just tell Mum to stop?' he pleaded. 'She's a *good* mum. She loves me. She really, really loves me. She doesn't want to hurt me. Maybe she just doesn't know it's wrong.'

Adam's sobs become compulsive, and my heart was breaking for him, but all I could do was hug him tighter and try to soothe him. I just didn't have the words to make this right.

Chapter 8

Friday

The plan – after a whispered conversation with John the previous evening – was to drop Adam off at school as if it were just another normal day. Which, of course, Adam already knew it wouldn't be, because he knew what he'd told me, making the whole thing a bit of a farce.

Still, there was nothing for it but to hold the previous line – that, yes, there really was a bug going round the hospital and, no, I couldn't promise him he'd see his mum the following night. And in the meantime, that he still needed to go to school.

There's a temptation, always, in such traumatic situations, to call normal life off and plunge in head first; focus fully on the problem and try to make things better. In reality, however, that was sometimes not the right thing to do. School mattered, and, for Adam, it would matter even more now. It was a constant – a place of routine and security in what would now become a scary and uncertain world.

And, perhaps understandably, today Adam really didn't want to go.

'I'm sorry, sweetie,' I told him when he appeared in the kitchen, still wearing his pyjamas, his face blotchy from crying and his shoulders slumped. 'But you really have to go in today. It's the last day of term, and you can't miss the last day of term, can you? Plus I have a whole ton of boring things to tick off my to-do list before my husband and son get back tonight. Come on, love,' I said, putting an arm around him and steering him back into the hall. 'It'll be fine once you get there. It'll take your mind off things.'

In reality, I wasn't sure it would do any such thing. But John had told me – another part of our whispered conversation – that he'd be on to Adam's head, was possibly speaking to him right now, so that he was in a position to offer Adam extra support. And though every nerve end was sparking, telling me to keep this poor child close to me, I knew it was the wrong thing. For all the intensity of the few days we'd spent together, I was still a stranger, whereas school represented everything he knew, from his teachers to his friends – whom he would really badly need now – to the dinner ladies and caretakers and the very fabric of the place.

And, meekly, eventually, Adam reappeared, dressed, and though he didn't eat much – no surprise there – he did manage a wan smile at the sight of the Kit Kat nestled atop his lunchtime cheese sandwich.

Then I took him to school, waved him off and contemplated the probable events of the day ahead – which began as I turned the car back into our drive, the display on my ringing phone saying *John Fulshaw*.

'Casey,' he said, 'right. Lots to tell you.' He sounded energised, like a car freewheeling down a hill, gathering momentum. As he would. This was his job and he was good at it. He was also unfettered by the emotional component, which was part of the job I had chosen to do. 'So. The first thing is that Adam has now been assigned his own social worker. Another Adam, as it happens, and he's been told what's going on.'

I locked the car as John talked, and headed indoors. 'That's good,' I said, even though it was also very sad; my little crisis placement had now become a 'case'.

'And, in light of what Adam disclosed to you last night about the pills,' John went on, 'my manager has reported the incident to the police, who have now been in touch with the hospital, and Mandy Conley is apparently going to be interviewed this morning.'

I tried to imagine Adam's mum, sitting in her side room, and a pair of uniformed officers appearing in the doorway. 'God, that's going to come as a shock to her.'

'I imagine it will,' John agreed. 'And what happens next will obviously depend on the outcome. I imagine she might be charged, but I'm told she's also being seen by a specialist, to establish whether she does seem to be suffering from Munchausen's.'

All so quick and efficient. And so sweeping. A full-stop

under a life. And perhaps a cure? I knew I'd be doing some more reading today.

'So in the meantime,' I said, 'you want me to hang on to Adam for a bit longer? Because, either way, he won't be able to be returned to her yet, will he?'

'No, he won't,' John confirmed, 'but it's a no to your first question. We won't be asking you to hold on to Adam.'

'Really?'

'A stroke of luck, for a change. Two strokes of luck, in fact. We've been able to get in touch with the uncle in Spain. He and his fiancée are getting a flight back tomorrow. Which is a godsend, because it means Adam has somewhere to stay.'

'That's allowed, is it? Even now he's in the system?'

'Yes, in this case. They're going to stay in Adam's house, which is obviously the most appropriate. And fine as long as Mrs Conley isn't there. Which she won't be. Not for a few days – they'll keep her in while they assess her. So at least Adam will be able to go home.'

'But what about tonight?'

'That's the second stroke of luck. He can stay with his next-door neighbour.'

'Wow, you have been busy.'

'Haven't we just. And she's more than happy to have him. She's a support worker, as it happens – not in this district, another one. Which means we're happy to leave Adam in her care till his uncle and auntie get here. She's also going to see if she can be assigned to his case – she's known him since he was a baby, apparently – which will obviously help enormously when it comes to moving on arrangements.'

'Moving on?' I asked, feeling more despondent by the minute. From right in the thick of things to out on the edges. That's pretty much what fostering felt like sometimes.

'Casey, you know how it's likely to go. With the best will in the world, I don't think it's likely that the uncle and aunt are just going to whisk the boy up and relocate him to Spain, even were it as simple as that now he's in care, which it's not. No, in all likelihood Adam will be going to mainstream carers for the time being. At least till it's established what the outcome with his mum is likely to be – whether she might eventually be in a position to care for him again.

'But what about us?' I heard myself saying. 'Why can't I – we – just hang on to him for now?'

'I knew you'd ask that,' John said, 'even though you already know the answer. There are plenty of lovely families we can billet Adam with, whereas specialist carers, for kids who have much more complex needs, are, as you already know, in very short supply. He might need permanent care, mightn't he? And you can't offer that and do what you do, can you? So to stay any longer with you would just make the transition more difficult.'

John was right, of course. As difficult as it was to accept, our hands were tied. Yes, we had Tyler long term, but he was older and had already shown he could cope with the challenges that specialist children brought to the family. To add Adam to the equation would be unfair on him, and would also limit the children we could take on.

So of course John was right. I already knew *all* this. It was just my usual reluctance to let go. But that was the nature of the job. And it *was* a job, one with guidelines and rules and, crappy as they sometimes felt, there was always sound reasoning behind them.

But it was with a heavy heart that I picked Adam up from school that day and told him my good friend John would be coming to collect him after tea.

Perhaps working on the assumption that if he didn't make any mention of what he'd told me the previous afternoon then perhaps I wouldn't, Adam took this on board with an uncomplicated whoop.

'Yes!' he said. 'Is Mum home? Is he coming to take me home to her?'

Which made the rest of what I had to tell him doubly awful.

I tried to keep it simple and imbue it with positives. And when I explained that he would be staying the night with his next-door neighbour, the spark of relief in his eyes reminded me that it was absolutely the right thing to do.

'So I'm going on a sleepover with Ellie? She used to babysit me when I was little,' he told me. 'When Mum was doing lots of lates.' Then his face fell. 'But for how long? And what's going to happen when Uncle Steve gets here? And what about Mum? Why can't she just come home?'

Again, I tried to explain that his mum was ill not just

with her appendicitis but also in her mind, and that the doctors were going to try to make her well again.

'But what if they *can't*?' he wanted to know. 'What then?'

And again, I couldn't give him an answer.

By the time John came to collect Adam, some 45 minutes later, we'd had a cuddle and he'd had a cry, and then he'd perked up a little – there was clearly a bond between him and his up till now distant uncle, and I could only hope it was one that could be strengthened. In the meantime I had to let this child go with as little ceremony and fuss as when I'd received him the previous Friday, so that he had a fighting chance of maintaining his composure.

I, on the other hand, managed no such small feat, letting the tears slide unchecked down my cheeks as I watched the pair of them walk down my front path, John with his briefcase and Adam with his little wheelie one, knowing that it was likely I would never see him again, and that in all probability I would for ever be associated with the memory of the most difficult and traumatic week of his life. I hoped he'd remember me fondly.

I was absolutely shattered emotionally, but there was no time to dwell on it. I had about ten minutes to get back up to the school to pick up Mike and Tyler, and I didn't want them to see me blubbing. I splashed my face with cold water, put on a bit of foundation and lip gloss – I hadn't seen Mike for over a week, after all. Then I dived back into my car and sped off.

I heard Tyler before I saw him. 'Muuuuum!' came the familiar yell – then the legs, then the rest of him, springing from the coach and sprinting across the school car park towards me. And I wasn't one bit embarrassed by him picking me up off the floor as he hugged me – something I'd long since stopped being able to do to him.

And then I saw Mike, hobbling down the coach steps to come and join us, and it really hit me just how much I'd missed them.

'Oh, it's so good to *see* you both,' I said as I kissed them both in turn. Then I slapped Mike on the chest with my car keys. 'And don't *ever* go away and break your bloody phone again. I was frantic!'

'Oh, Case, you're *such* a drama queen,' Mike said, laughing. 'It's *me* you should be feeling sorry for – me and my poor broken body.'

Tyler scraped an invisible bow across an imaginary violin on his shoulder. 'Yes,' he added. 'And don't we know it! What's that thing you're always saying, Mum? Don't make a drama out of a crisis? Well, Dad's made a *big* one, out of a *very* small crisis. He's not even got a sprain! Still, your boring week is over now. Normal service is resumed. Wait till you see my ten million photos!'

'And the lad? What was it, Adam?' Mike said, as he grabbed his holdall. 'Gone now?'

Gone now. I reached up to plant another kiss on my husband's cheek. 'Yes,' I said. Time enough to talk about it later.

Epilogue

Hindsight is a wonderful thing. In the weeks following Adam's departure it all fell into place for me, as I unpicked the events of that strange week. The appendicitis; it seemed the operation was completely straightforward, then the pain, and the constant need for extra medication – though it was never proven, it seemed clear that Adam's mother had been stockpiling painkillers, and that the move to a side room was a part of that too. And it was a morphine-based pain relief, which was why it made Adam so sick.

Adam's mother, thankfully, wasn't charged with any offence, but she was sectioned, and needed long-term, ongoing care for her Munchausen's disorder, which was diagnosed within a matter of days. And Adam did go into care, just as John had predicted. Just for three months, and with a family who had a ten-year-old son, with whom Adam became great friends and still sees.

And the uncle from Spain came to the rescue. After returning to Spain, he and his now wife sold their bar and returned to the UK, where they bought a house just a few miles from where Adam's mother returned to live, and once they moved in, took over care of their nephew.

They've since had their own child – a girl, whom Adam, I'm told, adores – and, with the help of counselling, he has adapted to his new life. He sees his mum regularly, and, though it's unlikely that she'll be able to care for him again, he's apparently happy and settled.

And also healthy. He still eats like a horse.

Rosie takes in Archie and his sister Bobbi after a
violent incident at their family home

She soon comes to suspect that something far more disturbing
lies in their past. When Archie tearfully discloses a shocking secret
that has left him and his sister traumatised, Rosie is horrified at
what she learns. She is determined to help the young siblings
find a forever home that will provide them with the love
and care they deserve.

BROKEN

ROSIE
LEWIS

An abandoned baby.

Separated from
her only family.

Searching for
a true home.

Taken

The heartbreaking case of Megan, a baby born
with a drug addiction and a cleft palate

Rosie tries to find new-born Megan a home, but she
has already found her 'forever mummy' in Rosie. Rosie
applies to adopt her, yet the system finds in favour of a
young couple. When Rosie learns that Megan's adoption
has broken down, will this little girl return to
her true 'forever home'?

TAKEN

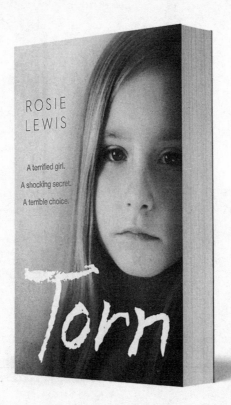

ROSIE
LEWIS

A terrified girl.
A shocking secret.
A terrible choice.

Torn

Rosie struggles when she agrees to take in
Taylor and her younger brother, Reece

She finds herself battling an unknown monster in
their past, as social media and the internet become a means
to control and manipulate the siblings while in her care.
And then a more sinister turn of events causes Rosie to dig
into their past, desperate to discover the truth before
her time with them is over and they must be
returned to their family.

TORN

The struggle to escape a life defined by family honour

With Rosie's support, thirteen-year-old Zadie gradually begins to settle into her new surroundings. But loyalty to her relatives and fear of bringing shame on her family keeps preventing Zadie from confessing the horrifying truth about her past. Will Rosie be able to persuade her to open up in time?

BETRAYED

ROSIE LEWIS

Trapped

The terrifying
true story of a
young girl's secret
world of abuse

The terrifying true story of a secret world of abuse

Phoebe, an autistic nine-year-old girl, is taken into
care when a chance comment to one of her teachers
alerts the authorities. After several shocking incidents
of self-harming and threats to kill, experienced foster
carer Rosie Lewis begins to suspect that there is
much more to Phoebe's horrific past than she
could ever have imagined.

TRAPPED

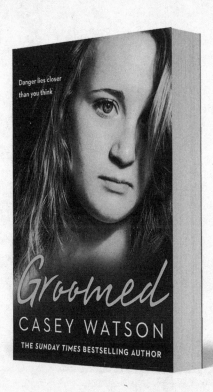

It's late on Friday night when
Casey gets a call from the
Emergency Duty Team

Fifteen-year-old Keeley has run away
from her long-term foster family and accused
her foster father of sexual abuse . . .

GROOMED

Adrianna arrives on Casey's doorstep with no possessions, no English and no explanation

It will be a few weeks before Casey starts getting the shocking answers to her questions . . .

RUNAWAY GIRL

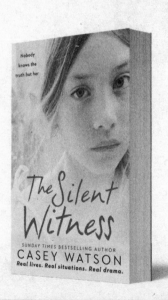

Bella's father is on a ventilator, fighting for his life, while her mother is currently on remand in prison, charged with his attempted murder

Bella is the only witness.

THE SILENT WITNESS

Flip is being raised by her alcoholic mother, and comes to Casey after a fire at their home

Flip has Foetal Alcohol Syndrome (FAS), but it soon turns out that this is just the tip of the iceberg . . .

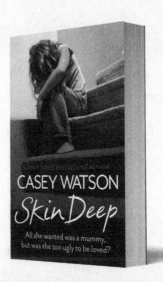

SKIN DEEP

Leo isn't a bad lad, but his frequent absences from school mean he's on the brink of permanent exclusion

Leo is clearly hiding something, and Casey knows that if he is to have any kind of future, it's up to her to find out the truth.

MUMMY'S LITTLE SOLDIER

What is the secret behind Imogen's silence?

Discover the shocking and devastating past of a child with severe behavioural problems.

THE GIRL WITHOUT A VOICE

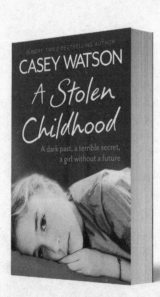

Kiara appears tired and distressed, and the school wants Casey to take her under her wing for a while

On the surface, everything points to a child who is upset that her parents have separated. The horrific truth, however, shocks Casey to the core.

A STOLEN CHILDHOOD

A teenage mother and baby in need of a loving home

At fourteen, Emma is just a child herself – and one who's never been properly mothered.

A LAST KISS FOR MUMMY

Eleven-year-old Tyler has stabbed his stepmother and has nowhere to go

With his birth mother dead and a father who doesn't want him, what can be done to stop his young life spiralling out of control?

NOWHERE TO GO

A young girl secretly caring for her mother

Abigail has been dealing with pressures no child should face. Casey has the difficult challenge of helping her to learn to let go.

Two boys with an unlikely bond

With Georgie and Jenson, Casey is facing her toughest test yet.

Abused siblings who do not know what it means to be loved

With new-found security and trust, Casey helps Ashton and Olivia to rebuild their lives.

LITTLE PRISONERS

Branded 'vicious and evil', eight-year-old Spencer asks to be taken into care

Casey and her family are disgusted: kids aren't born evil. Despite the challenges Spencer brings, they are determined to help him find a loving home.

TOO HURT TO STAY

Five-year-old Justin was desperate and helpless

Six years after being taken into care, Justin has had 20 failed placements. Casey and her family are his last hope.

THE BOY NO ONE LOVED

A damaged girl haunted by her past

Sophia pushes Casey to the limits, threatening the safety of the whole family. Can Casey make a difference in time?

CRYING FOR HELP

AVAILABLE AS E-BOOK ONLY

Jade and Scarlett, seventeen-year-old twins, share a terrible secret

Can Casey help them come to terms with the truth and rediscover their sibling connection?

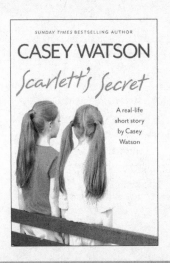

SCARLETT'S SECRET

Nathan has a sometime alter ego called Jenny who is the only one who knows the secrets of his disturbed past

But where is Jenny when she is most needed?

NO PLACE FOR NATHAN

Angry and hurting, eight-year-old Connor is from a broken home

As streetwise as they come, he's determined to cause trouble. But Casey is convinced there is a frightened child beneath the swagger.

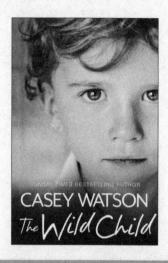

THE WILD CHILD

Six-year-old Darby is naturally distressed at being removed from her parents just before Christmas

And when the shocking and sickening reason is revealed, a Happy New Year seems an impossible dream as well . . .

THE LITTLE PRINCESS

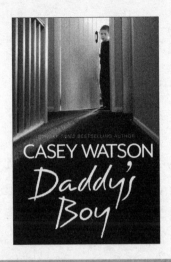

Moving Memoirs

Stories of hope, courage and the power of love…

If you loved this book, then you will love our
Moving Memoirs eNewsletter

Sign up to…

- Be the first to hear about new books

- Get sneak previews from your favourite authors

- Read exclusive interviews

- Be entered into our monthly prize draw to win one
  of our latest releases before it's even hit the shops!

Sign up at

www.moving-memoirs.com